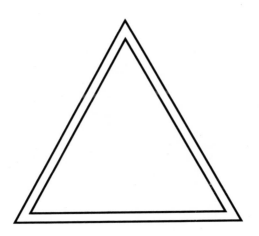

This book was written with the permission and the blessing
of Joao de Deus.

This book is dedicated to the Healing Entities of Abadiânia.

I thank them with all my heart for their willingness to communicate.

May their message – that we are all connected – be understood
and honoured throughout the human world

Imprint

© 2014 by Silverline Publishing
production: BoD – Books on Demand
Cover- and book design: Anja Jakob
Editing: Birgit Groll, Benediktbeuern;
www.birgit-groll-coaching.de
Translation : Frauke Watson

ISBN: 978-9962-702-06-1

contact: Sylvia Leifheit
www.sylvialeifheit.de
contact@silverline-publishing.com

∞

In memory
of Chico Xavier

Index

Chapter 1 - Interviews

Chapter 2- Practical

∞

8

For several decades, the Brazilian town of Abadiânia has been the home of medium and healer Joao de Deus (John of God).

With the help of 'spiritual entities' that incorporate into Joao, he has been able to heal thousands of people of their physical and spiritual illnesses. The treatments that these entities administer through Joao de Deus come either in the form of visible or invisible operations.

In Joao's house, the "Casa", there are rooms with different functions. Depending on the visitors' needs, they can wait in one of several lines in order to be seen by Joao. Then there is the "current", a room where people sit and meditate for hours in order to maintain the healing current generated by Joao de Deus and his host of spiritual entities. In the room of the "crystal beds", patients can lie down and receive gentle energetic healing.

The results of countless healings performed by, among others, Dom Ignacio de Loyola, Dr. Augusto and Dr. Valdivino through the medium Joao de Deus have been corroborated by the findings of western science.

I myself visited Abadiânia for the first time in May 2012 in order to seek healing for an eye problem. Even at this first visit I was told by an entity that I would be developing a spiritual gift.

I could not make heads or tails of this announcement at the time because the entity did not offer any more information. But during a "crystal bed" treatment a few days later, I suddenly began to "receive" complete and clear sentences.

The entity called Dom Ignacio explained to me that I had received the gift to communicate with the spiritual entities. He asked me to use this gift in order to enter into contact with the "healing entities of Abadiânia."

Through my ability to communicate with them, the entities would have the opportunity to answer questions about their nature and the way that they worked. This type of communication was something completely new in this place. Up to that point, the entities had only communicated nonverbally through their operations and spiritual healings.

During the interviews, it quickly became clear that the entities were able to supply important comments about the people's actions and attitudes. On the one hand, these are comments about the right attitude when visiting the Casa in Abadiânia, but on the other hand they are appeals to all of us to live our life in the awareness of healing. Many entities also offer interesting comments about the social, political and religious institutions of human civilization in these "interviews".

This book is the first one of a series about interviews with spiritual entities. More books will follow in the near future.
I hope and wish that the messages expressed in these interviews may contribute to raising and supporting our awareness of the spiritual worlds.

Sylvia Leifheit

2014

∞

Introduction

The purpose of our existence is to experience life joyfully and, hopefully, to give nothing but love. Every feeling that is not accompanied by love, every action that did not arise from a loving heart is not in resonance with the cosmos and will produce resonances that may result in illness or other negative experiences.

But there is absolutely no reason not to act in harmony with the universal laws. Not even oblivion, caused by the change of perception while transitioning from the spiritual state into incarnation, can take the burden of responsibility off our shoulders – on the contrary. All human beings are responsible for themselves and their own actions. Hence all human beings must walk the path of enlightenment and, through this, the path of energetic cleansing all by themselves. Nobody can take this burden from us. The only thing we can do is ask for cosmic assistance, but this will only be given if we are truly ready for it.

*

About the author

I have been travelling strange worlds since early childhood. I often "went outside of my body", feeling as if a suit of heavy armour was removed from me; I was light as a feather and free from the restrictions of physical existence. When I returned, it always felt as if thousands of tons of lead were again encasing my body and everything became constricted and painfully hot. Very early on, I began to write down my adventures in those other worlds of perception.

But during the next few years, as the pressure of the "human army", as I like to call it, increased, calling on me to conform to the rules and regulations of earthly existence, I duly submitted to the strictures imposed on me. As I gradually gave up my freedom of thought, my ability to travel other levels of awareness began to diminish along with it. Until there came a day when I had all but forgotten about it.

Then suddenly, in the middle of a perfectly ordinary night, my soul suddenly remembered this state of freedom. A door that had all but closed opened again and I swore to myself never again to accept as my own perception the feeling of separation that is second nature to my fellow humans.
In my own perception, there never had been a separation between human beings and spiritual entities; on the contrary. I saw the humans as a kind of preschoolers who tried in their foggy and rather unaware way to dominate the world when they did not even know their alphabet. They, in turn, were suspicious of my own way of thinking and acting – until I gave up even discussing it. Human heartlessness comes in many guises and I had grown tired of provoking it. So, in my turn, I acted as

if I was just another dutiful foot soldier in the human army, never asking questions of my own. On the other hand, however, I quietly worked on developing my gift.

So I lived in constant communication with fairies, leprechauns, angels, Masters, teachers, guardian spirits, the deceased, as well as highly vibrating energy gestalts that no longer have a form – and many, many other forms of being. They are and will always be parts of the whole, just as we are parts of the same whole.

My driving force is curiosity, most of all curiosity about how the cosmos works. Like a kind of spiritual scientist I use my gift of communicating with the spiritual energies in order to learn from them. I never found any of the things I write or will ever write in someone else's books. I quickly gave up looking for answers there, for I have never found in them such a wealth of explanations for the true wholeness of the cosmos as I have learned through contacting the spiritual energies.

The journey is the reward – and so my inquiring mind has ever grown inside me until one day I stood before Joao de Deus to seek for answers for my eye that were growing weaker and weaker; answers that even the spiritual world around me had not been able to give so far. So I hoped that I would find help here in Abadiânia. And I did receive help – but as I know now, my eyes only served as a type of anchor that dragged me in the direction my inner being wanted me to go. Because toward the end of my first trip to Joao and his spiritual helpers, this entity inside me had told me: "You will develop a gift."

This may not sound particularly "special" to some of my readers, but this little sentence meant the world to me. Because finally, I knew that there was someone who not only recognized my ability but who also validated it! I felt like a child who had been resigned to being lonely for the rest of her life, and who was suddenly taken by the hand by someone who knew without words what was the matter with me. This was by no means just a phrase for me; it turned into the growing resolve to stand up for my gift and to live it more visibly.

From that moment on, my attitude began to change with every step and every answer from the spiritual world. I developed into a person who consciously and continuously lived her connection with other spiritual levels and their inhabitants.

This led to the publication of my first book about all the knowledge that I had gained up to that point. *Das 1x1 des Seins* (The basics of being) is a synopsis of all this knowledge and was meant to cast a glimpse into the eternity that had been shown to my inquiring spirit ever since I could think. Everyone who is interested in the fundamental questions about the cosmos will find answers there.

But in order to provide my readers with a basic guideline, I will now give a small introduction into the cosmic laws as they were taught to me by the spiritual entities on the higher levels. This can help to put the messages given in this book into a clearer context. I suggest that you read this before the interviews with the entities of Abadiânia.

Introduction to the cosmic laws

The cosmos is energy.
All existence is a form of energy and is therefore eternally changing; energy cannot disappear, it just transforms and with that, changes form.

Cosmic energy is conscious.
Unlike energy produced by machines, it came from the one source and will return to it again and again.

This source is a power that cannot be described with words.
It is pure consciousness without form.

The soul is the "first form" the source energy takes on. It uses the different energy states of the cosmos to develop its form by adding experience.

The energies choose different forms in order to gain experience. Incarnation into a human organism is one of these forms.

Energy can be contaminated. Pure energy is conscious of the interconnectedness of all things; contaminated energy loses this perception according to its degree of impurity.

Contamination can happen through the process of incarnation, through eating the wrong food or clinging to the wrong patterns of thought. All of this can block or obstruct the flow of cosmic energy in the human body.

These blockages/contaminations can then cause all sorts of illnesses of a spiritual or physical nature.

Cleansing/purification of the physical body and the energy flow is therefore an indispensable part of our personal responsibility.

Balancing of the energy is an integral part of the purification. Healing can only start where balance has been re-established.

The actual healing process is initiated by the re-establishment of a healthy energy flow in the body.

The health of the human body is dependent on the quality of connectedness with the source in order to receive energy. When the cosmic connection is strengthened, the body's life force and with that, the power of self-healing will increase.

Every being, every plant and every "form" in the cosmos has emerged from the source and is eternally connected with it. This connection is eternal but when the consciousness is contaminated, it can no longer be consciously perceived. This then leads to negative feelings such as depression, loneliness, fear and hate.

To the degree that our body is cleansed, our perception will improve and the symptoms will disappear. At the same time, our perception of interconnectedness will improve and the spiritual world will become visible.

The cosmos is boundless. Still, it may be helpful for humans to have a rough idea about the "most important" states of being. I have been able to list them according to my perceptions up to this point.

∞

When perception becomes blurred through a contaminated mind, our creative power and our free will create the ego. Then, a vicious cycle will begin; the ego will lead us away from the feeling of connectedness into the feeling of separation.

Every form of cosmic energy has consciousness and free will.

The experience of love is an experience of connectedness. If you love, you are connected; if you are connected, you heal.

You will find a more detailed discussion of these matters in my book *Das 1x1 des Seins* (The basics of being).

17

The spiritual worlds

The Source
It is the sphere behind, before, above and inside of all matter. It is the state of highest vibration and can be reached from all directions. Every form of energy can attain the energy state of the source, i.e. return to source.

Since all forms of energy are always connected to the source, it cannot be categorized as a spiritual level; rather, it is an all-pervading force.

Emanating, as are all things, from the source are the levels of beings; the spiritual levels or worlds.

The 7th world

It is the first level of form, where smaller units emerge from the formless sea of cosmic energy. The individual "soul" gestalt emerges.

The 6th world
This is the level where individuation has progressed so far that those souls can be contacted. It is the plane of the "Wise Brotherhood", with whom I am keeping very close contact and whose knowledge I treasure.

The 5th world
This is the level of stabilisation, the realm of the Guardian and Master entities. They remove cosmic impurities that are not connected to a soul. They balance dissonant energies and re-establish cosmic harmony. King Solomon is one of the entities working from this level. The Wise Brotherhood will work together with the entities on this level if necessary.

∞

The 4th world

Here, there are the "Master entities of the special Qualities". They archive, stabilise and help when needed. Most of the entities of Abadiânia work from this level and the Wise Brotherhood call on this energy in order to work. The entirety of this huge energy field is what the human beings know as "white energy".

The 3rd world

This is the level of the Ascended Masters that we know by name.

The 2nd world

This is the world of those energies that humans like to call angels.

The 1st world

This is the spiritual level of the deceased, of human souls who transitioned into the spiritual world. Here, there are lighter as well as darker areas. Whichever area the soul will perceive depends on the level of purity at the time of its transition.

Instruction leaflet

Although I wrote down the answers by hand, I have taped all the interviews in order to be able to retain the answers that were writing themselves through my hand. I was speaking them out loud at the same time, because during these interviews I am in a different state of perception, similar to a light trance– and unfortunately, this means that afterwards I cannot remember any of the answers that were given. It is therefore essential that I tape the messages in order to transmit them exactly as they were given. So you are reading the dialogue exactly as it happened. I will not and must not change any of the entities' answers because I am just the channel and not an editing filter. At times it may feel awkward to read a spoken and unedited dialogue, but at the same time it allows you to get a feel for the entity that speaks.

The information given here about energy, spirits, the deceased, death, the afterlife and many other things are perceived quite differently by the entities that provided it. Therefore you as a reader need to bring to this a certain readiness to question the familiar structures.

- Spiritual entities do not feel in the same way as human beings do, but they do have feelings.

- Spiritual entities do not judge in the way that humans do; they are the sum of their experience and they talk to us from the point of view of the memory of the emotions that went with a specific experience. I was often quite overcome by the force of the emotions that they communicated to me. I have tried to integrate my feelings into the dialogue in order to let you participate more closely. This will allow you to connect with these entities even more easily.

- Although spiritual entities perceive things from a higher perspective, they are not omniscient. So the views they express in this book may therefore surprise some readers who have learnt to think otherwise. It is a common fallacy to believe that these entities can see a person's past, present and future. They explain to us in their own words why this is not possible. They simply read the energy around a person, no more and no less.

- "The language of the soul does not need words" – this quote by Dr. Augusto explains why it was sometimes quite difficult for the entities to choose the right words for their message. Communication happens on many levels simultaneously; so at times they chose to transmit an image or a specific emotion rather than words. But since this was a spoken dialogue that I was supposed to write down for you to read, I sometimes needed to ask again and again in order to get to the essence of the message. It sometimes took a little time until we found the right words, but it also served to strengthen my connection to the entity.

- When you open yourself up, you will be able to establish a connection to each and every spiritual entity speaking in this book.

I hope that in this book, you may find many inspiring insights and maybe the answers to some of your questions that have long gone unanswered. If you are truly ready to open, the answers will come to you!

∞

Interviews

∞

24

Dom Ignacio de Loyola - Saint Ignatius from Loyola

**"For those who believe, no proof is necessary.
For those who disbelieve, no amount of proof is sufficient."**

Many biographers divide his life into four phases:

First phase – worldly troubles

Being born into a noble family, the bright and able-bodied youth spent
much of his time around the Castilian court. During this phase he was
of a warlike inclination, bent on valour and noble deeds. During the war
against the French he had been defending the city of Pamplona as a military commander, when he was hit by a cannon ball which broke one of
his legs and severely wounded the other. When the French took the for-
tress, Ignacio and his men were taken prisoners. He was subsequently
released for his bravery in battle. An operation in order to redress his
broken bones brought him close to death. He received the last rites, but
did recover. However, he now walked with a limp.

Second phase - spiritual reorientation

In order not to stay disabled, Ignacio underwent a second, no less painful operation. During his long convalescence he read voraciously. The
only books that were available in the Castle, however, were about the

life of Christ and the life of the saints. This changed Ignacio profoundly; he gradually rejected material goods, his ambition for fame and his longing for courtly life, directing his thoughts instead towards spirituality. As a consequence, he left his family, changing his noble trappings for the simple garments of a beggar. Not surprisingly, he was mocked mercilessly, being called "brother sack" because of his shapeless clothing. Yet his noble and magnanimous mind did not fail to impress the people who came to him for solace. Soon he took up his mission as a religious preacher.

Third phase – late realization of his religious studies
Initially in Barcelona and later in Salamanca, Ignacio dedicated his life to religious studies, preaching and the conversion of sinners. Soon, he attracted the attention of the Spanish Inquisition but having been able to acquit himself of the accusations raised against him, Ignacio was allowed to go free and carry on preaching. He went on to Paris to continue his studies and there he received a Masters' degree and "Latinized" his name into Ignatius. He soon acquired quite a following, of whom Pedro Fabre, Francisco Xavier and Diego Lanez are the most well-known.

Fourth phase – the founding of the Society of Jesus
The saintliness of Ignatius de Loyola soon became a byword, especially among the young people who began to seek him out for spiritual guidance. In 1534, he founded the first Society of Jesus with his faithful disciples, also known as the Jesuit Order. Ignatius had the gift of healing and often performed veritable miracles on his supplicants. His disciples also preached in many public places in Italy and in 1540, after several years of waiting, Pope Paul III finally ratified the Jesuit Order.
Ignatius de Loyola fulfilled a great mission as a preacher; his order thrived in Europe and soon he sent missionaries to all the continents. In

Brazil, the Society of Jesus led by Padre Manoel da Nobrega has had a great historical impact in the New World.

(Source: Spiritual Healing, Ismar E. Garcia)

Interview

Dear entity that we humans call Dom Ignacio, I am happy to make contact with you. You have given me the task to write this book... Now it is time, I am here and you are welcome to begin transmitting your messages to mankind.

> *I am happy that you have heeded my call. Humans need purification.*

And this space is a very pure space, right?

> *I have got tired of the suffering of mankind and have therefore been seeking for a space, which gave/gives me the opportunity to incorporate.*

Dom Ignacio, how am I to visualize this from your perspective? How does one find such a place? As a human, we imagine the spirit flying over the earth, seeking and seeking... how did this work with you?

> *When humans seek, they have to travel a lot, but as a spiritual being you can be everywhere at the same time.*

Still, it took a while to find this place... can you describe the process? Did you just wish for it and then it was there, or how did this happen?

> *The energy of the place is very good, which is why I started to observe this place.*

∞

Dear Dom Ignacio, please help me to clarify for us humans what exactly you perceive. You are on this other level and you wish to help the humans. You have got the energy that allows you to incorporate and then you seek this place, you find it immediately because you can be everywhere at the same time and you start to observe it. But: in what 'time'? How exactly does this "observing" happen?

When the spirit has acquired a certain aim, it begins to materialise this direction. It is impossible to measure this process in terms of time because time does not exist on these levels.

This brings me to the next question: You do not have such as thing as time, yet you experience every day on earth in order to help. Which would mean that you would at least experience a certain manner of time when you are there?

29

Only when a spirit obtains permission to enter a human body, only then does it experience time. Otherwise, it is impossible.

As a spiritual entity, you do not experience time, but you still observe a linear progression of events, right?

Yes.

So you do not experience past, present and future simultaneously, but there is a sequence of events, it just is not measurable in terms of time?

Yes.

∞

Dear Dom Ignacio, you founded the Jesuit order during that lifetime. As far as I understand, the Jesuit order closely cooperated with the church at that time. Did you see behind the curtain of negativity then?

No. At that time, the church was the only way to obtain eternal life. I was not aware at that time that the church exercised such a negative influence on the people.

How do you perceive the influence of this institution now? Has your image of the church changed at all?

I now perceive the church as negative in many aspects because it holds the people down and makes them culpable. The energy it emanates is not expansive but restrictive.

30

Since you now realise this from your new, clearer perspective, how important, would you say, is expansion as opposed to restriction?

A soul's expansion is a prerequisite for its health. Unfortunately, I have only come to this realisation after that lifetime.

Could it be said that the restrictive human belief patterns around rules and regulations, retribution and sin are one of the causes for many illnesses?

Alas, yes. The religions in your world all have a very restrictive effect on the human spirit. The only real religion is the love of life itself. Humans create their destiny through their actions but they should be free to do this and not full of fear.

∞

Dear Dom Ignacio, then we have a problem all over the earth. To this day, children are born into the frightening, constrictive structures of these religions. Humans who freely follow their hearts are very, very rare. How can we change that?

Humans need light and love in order to get healthy. You can bring them light. And love...

Dear Dom Ignacio, we have the opportunity to "plant" messages into this book. How can we make people change their ideas?

Humans need to realise that love is the key to everything. If they realise that, they can heal their causes with love or avoid, through love, becoming ill. Love is the essence of healing. Fear is the essence of illness.

31

Dear Dom Ignacio, you have created the Spiritual Exercises in your lifetime. Do you still stand by them or would you change or amend them?

I would change some things because quite a few things are not right.

Dear Dom Ignacio, I can get hold of a copy and then we can work on them together. If you like, I would be happy to work on them together with you, how about it?

I would be very happy to.

Dear Dom Ignacio, I would like to go into your lifetime now... You had this accident and then you started on your spiritual path. You have spent

∞

your entire life without loving a woman or having a family. Is this something you regret or was this exactly right for you?

I do not wish to answer this question because I have chosen this path with a goal in mind. And I have reached this goal.

What I really mean is to find out whether this path you have followed… to renounce the love between man and woman… whether this is the only right path to obtain this spiritual goal, or whether you think that this goal could also be reached together with a woman.

This path was the only one for me because the release of human attachments is one of the most important steps towards the liberation of the soul.

32 Could you say that you obtained complete purification in your life? Or how else would you call this process, for which the release of attachments was such an important step?

My life was dedicated to the release of impurities acquired in previous lives and the beginning of a spiritual form. My current form, for me, is the most appropriate because it can exist without losing energy and without "aging".

Is there something that makes you sad in your current activity?

I am sad when I see that the humans do not want to heal. I cannot understand how a soul can choose a path and then fail to take the crucial steps.

∞

Dom Ignacio, I put it to you that it is not the soul that refuses to take these steps but the ego. What do you say to this?

The humans have lost connection and that makes my work very hard sometimes.

Are there many who do not want to heal?

Yes, alas.

Since we are here, is there something that you can give them in order to allow them to remove their ego from the path to healing?

I want to tell them that the soul does not know fear. Release, freedom, is the destiny of all souls.

33

That means that we tell them to do their utmost in order to expand and to try and overcome fear wherever it appears. Right?

Yes.

It is really this simple, it is just fear which drives the people towards illness?

Yes. Please try to make them understand that their fears are the viruses of the spirit. Humans still don't understand that love heals everything.

I have a small question on my own behalf. I once experienced a spirit "walking into" me. I was aware of his presence, he moved very quickly as if he was flying. And I felt how determined he was to enter me. I felt quite set upon and I did not allow it. Is this how you operate?

This was the spirit of a deceased person who in his desperation was trying to use your body as a channel in a disrespectful manner. All of us here work quite differently. In our highly elevated levels, there is no will to manipulate another; we come when we are called. Joao calls us.

Where do you dwell? How can I visualize you?

We are always in our sphere.

Where is this sphere?

34

The fourth level.

As far as I can remember, this is the level of the Ascended Masters, right?

Yes, this level is the level of the Ascended Masters.

Can all of you incorporate?

No, this is a quality that only a few of us choose to carry out.

How did it come to pass that other entities of this level are also exercising their influence on us?

Our work here creates resonances, which are perceived by other en-

lightened entities, who then also wish to come and help.

How do you perceive the earth and the humans from this level?

I cannot see the humans but I feel their force. The humans need more devotion because they are falling out of their connection with the spiritual world.

Can you feel and see how humankind is doing at this time?

Humankind is on the path into darkness.

Dear Dom Ignacio, many books have told us that the year 2012 marks the point at which this process has reached its end point and is turning around. Can you see a movement in that direction, can you see whether our movement into darkness has changed direction?

35

Humankind is moving faster than ever into darkness and by no means into the light.

What will you do when Joao is no longer on earth?

I will find another place to heal.

Will you continue to live in the spiritual world or will you try to incorporate?

If they call me, I will come, but I myself would never try to occupy a body of my own accord.

What has moved you most during your lifetime, what has brought you closer to becoming pure spirit?

I was at the stage where I no longer wished to experience the mundane. I no longer found any fulfilment in planning the next battle or experiencing the next drama. Through abandoning the human perception, I embarked upon several new paths. The books of Jesus allowed me to see the world through different eyes. The first inklings of the experience of love I felt there brought me a kind of fulfilment I had never experienced before. This made it clear to me that I was no longer able to gain fulfilment though material things but only through subtle, or rather, spiritual things. Then I started to try to familiarise myself with the feeling of no longer having a body and these exercises led me closer to my goal. The goal was to no longer adhere to material things in any shape or form but to live a life of love.

So you wanted to be nothing but love.

Yes.

And this without attachment?

Yes.

What was the hardest thing for you?

I could not always live this love because my mind was clouded by human needs. But I channelled all my energy into this desire and during my transition from body to spirit this wish materialised as

potential. I was allowed to choose whether I wanted to incarnate again or to stay in the spiritual state in order to continue to love from this position.

Can you describe a little what it looks like where you are now, what exactly do you perceive?

It is very light and powerful here, I like that very much.

Are you alone there or are the other beings there as well?

I am still connected to the other entities. But I am relatively undisturbed here.

Do you feel the urge to explore other levels of being?

37

I want to stay here forever; this is the perfect place for me. But I know about the transmutation of energies. And if I should wish to transmute, it could be that I can answer your question in the affirmative.

I have asked you, dear Dom Ignacio, what makes you sad. But is there anything that makes you happy?

A beautiful question. I am always full of joy when a human being has experienced a healing. This transformation is like a birth and I am the midwife.

Are you experiencing a male or female identity where you are or are you genderless?

I am genderless. I have cast off the identity of gender.

Do you happen to know whether you have incarnated on earth before?

I have incarnated many times before, but these experiences were never really happy.

And this is why you manifested the wish never to incarnate again, is that right?

Yes.

Would you like to tell me what happens during the operation?

I would be happy to. During the operation, the people will be subjected to a kind of energy shower. This supplies the soul with energy, which it would otherwise acquire, too, but very slowly, through meditation or other loving exercises.

When people come to you and don't heal, is this because they have not given permission?

These people have given the permission but their ingrained thought patterns and feelings always block the healing process whenever they are asked to take a new path.

So they block their healing at the crucial moment?

Yes.

38

Would you like to offer some advice to these people?

That their suffering will not diminish when they continue to walk the old paths. That their fear with become their destiny.

Dear Dom Ignacio, this means that we will give the responsibility for their own life back into these people's hands through showing them again that they are indeed responsible?

It is especially the personal responsibility that is very important to me. The people have forgotten how to find responsibility in themselves, because the world religions are all faulty when it comes to this subject. All of them seek the cause of the problems outside and never teach us to seek the causes inside of us.

What has changed in terms of how people deal with religion nowadays?

In the old days, the people disdained the path of love, concentrating instead on their connection to the church. I am saying this because in those days, I met very few people who considered love as the highest good.

But this is the same today.

It may be the same in your time but I can only answer for my own time.

I understand. Was it hard for you to find people of like mind in those days?

Yes. I was very alone for a long time. But I used this time for my inner cleansing.

Would you like to share how important this cleansing is?

This process is especially important. For no material power is as pure as the spirit. But at the same time, the spirit is the cause for lost connection.

About the subject of operations: What do people have to bear in mind for the time after the operation?

This time is important in order to harmonize the regained soul energy with the body.

40   And this is why we should refrain from too much movement?

Yes.

Why the rule about the forty days of abstinence from sexual activity?

Sexual energy is very different from the spiritual energy we work with. These two energies block each other. This is why it is important to adhere to this rule in order to heal.

But people have done research and found out that sexual energy can also be very beneficial. It can energize and remove blockages. What is your view on that?

This is true, but it is not helpful to our kind of healing. Blockages

in the body absorb and bind power that can be released with sexual
activity. But we are working with the structure of the soul, which is
much subtler than the structure of the physical body.

How come that after your operations, there are visible cuts on the organs?

These are energetic cuts; they are not real cuts but only a result of
the energetic acceleration of the soul.

Are there different degrees? Do you use different degrees of acceleration depending on what the person can tolerate?

Yes. We vary our dosage according to the actual potential of the
soul.

41

How do you decide whether or not to intervene? Is it the request or your
insight into the energetic structure of the people in question?

The request is the decisive factor.
This is always the case when action is taken in the cosmos.
The person's request shifts the soul's energy to the speed that it can
tolerate. The acceleration is always in accordance with the spirit.

Would you like to tell the people something about this? We now have
the opportunity to get everyone who reads this attuned to wishing and
asking for the right thing...

With pleasure! Please communicate to them that we always act in
resonance with their innermost wishes. It is therefore important

∞

that you state these wishes clearly. Do not just ask for healing but also for the healing of the causes.

Dear Dom Ignacio, in most cases it seems that most people don't really know the causes.

Yes.

So how do we help them to find those causes?

They can do this by meditating. We feel into their energy and show them the feelings and images that block them. This perception is the call to action, to state their wishes clearly.

Do the entities continue to work on you even after the operation?

42

Sometimes, yes. It depends on whether this is wished. You have to imagine this like an onion. The energy penetrates layer after layer. This takes time.

I felt after one operation that something was removed from my light body.

Yes, that is right, that is when fears in the shape of brown energy fields are removed.

And after that, I felt an energy ball in my aura, which seemed to be of a completely different quality?

That was the ball of accelerating energy.

∞

What did they do with this orb?

The orb became a part of you.
This orb became your energy.

Why did this orb take shape in front of me?

This is part of the operation.

But please explain briefly how this process unrolls.

This energy was removed from you, then it was cleansed and in the cleansed state placed back into you.

How does this energy come out? Just like that, or how do you do it?

This happens because of the high energy of the place. The energy inside you is open... and therefore it becomes visible to us and can be more easily cleansed.

But doesn't this cleansing take place inside us instead of outside of us?

Yes, it happens inside you. But your high sensitivity made you perceive it this way.

So you were really inside me but I perceived it as if it happened outside of me, right?

Yes, that is the correct description.

And what happened then, when I felt as if something went into me?

That was your cleansed energy.

But when the onion layer has been opened like that, doesn't it increase the danger of taking on negative energies again?

That is indeed a problem, which is why we ask the people to leave this place immediately. The casa is full of negative energy fields in those places where the energy is not at its highest.

Okay, can you share something here that helps people to protect themselves against that?

Yes, I can. Please protect yourselves by crossing yourself in an upwards direction in front of your body.

That brings me to a question. Since time immemorial, people have been crossing themselves in a downward direction. I have learned from the Rosicrucians that the cross is meant to go the other way round. Can you share your experience?

The people always cross themselves the wrong way around. The cross does not point downwards but upwards.

And then you tell the people that their medication will be adjusted for them here. Is this right?

Yes.

How does this work exactly?

Every medication is in a neutral state. It is the inherent energy of the person who wishes for healing that programs the drug.

Then it is not you who programs the drug but the people themselves, right?

Exactly.

It there anything else to bear in mind after such an operation?

The energy during the operation is many times higher than you have known before. This is like flying when you have only ever walked.

Please tell me about the role of Joao Deus during such an operation. Does he do something, or the entity that is inside him?

45

No. The entity that is incorporated in him only accompanies this process, it does not transform the energy.

Did you have spiritual perception as an incorporated human, in so far as you could talk to entities like I do?

I could not do that but I had a feeling inside me that guided me.

So you followed your intuition.

Since I have known you, no other human being has been able to communicate with entities of our level as well as you do.

That is a pity really, because surely there must have been many mediums here.

That may be, but they have a different kind of perception.

Back to the operations, can you tell me anything else about them?

When we operate, it is usually a very intense process. The people are more or less aware of this process. But this is only due to their awareness.

What can we tell them about this? How can they manage to be conscious when they are going to be operated upon?

Giving permission to call the entities is a big step towards awareness. We are all there because of our awareness, which we consciously direct.

That means that one of you is inside Joao and the others are there in consciousness, right?

You have put this correctly. The entity, which speaks through Joao is also with us but its consciousness is with Joao. All the others are working on the human's soul through their awareness.

I have a question concerning the crystals. I am finding many crystals here but they are all impure. Does it matter whether they are impure or not? What do the crystals do?

You have perceived correctly. A pure crystal is the most precious stone there is. It is extremely rare to find such purity and it is many times more potent than impure crystals.

Back to the place where this is all happening: So the humans are not supposed to read or do anything after their operation. Can you explain to me why this is so?

This is meant to prevent the many different ways of distraction from healing. Reading or other activitiesy set thought patterns in motion that are supposed to sleep at this time.

Are people already operated upon in the current or is at least a sort of operation taking place there?

In there, the first layers of the soul are being expanded and cleansed. This is like a preliminary step. And this is where you are provided with the images which are meant to help you to formulate the right request for the operation.

47

Is your number constant or are there also new entities joining you?

There is always the same number of entities, but I have observed that travelling entities drop by from time to time.

But they have to be of a high vibration, don't they? I mean, pure entities.

Yes. The purity of an entity is a prerequisite in order to get to this place.

Is there an entity to which you have a special affinity?

∞

Dr. Valdivino. He has become a good friend because he also lives many of my connections.

Which connection is there between you and King Solomon?

His energy is very high. I am curious as to what you will learn from him. He is very much enveloped in protective energies because his vibration is really very high.

The higher an entity vibrates, the more it radiates and this radiation protects it, right?

Exactly so.

Will you name a place in the Casa that should take on a higher importance for people?

The chapel, because it is there that wishful energies will be fulfilled.

Why is this?

This is because of the purity of the chapel.

What do you think of the crystal beds?

The crystal beds are very good in order to be cleansed in a gentle manner, but it is better to have an operation.

What is the reason behind visible operations?

The visible operations help the people to better understand that we are there.

And what exactly happens when Joao scratches the eyes?

It is not the eye he touches. It is the layer of the soul which leads into the eyes. He cleanses this layer. The visual operation is in no way better than the energetic operation.

Okay, I thank you very much and I am looking forward to next time. Thank you.

You are welcome.

The white orbs

Interview

I asked who would like to introduce themselves next and a cleansing entity came forth.

Dear cleansing entity, are you by yourself?

No, we are legion.

Should I talk to you personally or to all of you?

Please talk to all of us.

Are you exclusively transforming energy?

Yes. Energy is transformation.

How do you work with the energy fields? How am I to imagine this? What exactly do you do there; can you describe this?

It is difficult to describe.

Please try.

You have to imagine this as a shower of love. The energy fields are submerged in transcendent cosmic love energy by our energy.

Submerged how?

We take out parts of the impurity, then we bring them into this energy and then we put them back in.

This means that we are without this energy for a short time?

Yes, without that part.

And what if you leave these energy parts out completely? I mean, just take them out and keep them out?

That does not work because they are part of the soul.

51

Can you provide an image for that? I suppose it is like a pie and you take out a segment?

You have got it.

And if a part were missing, what could happen?

This would not be good because the soul would be unstable and not healthy. The part that was taken out must be brought back under all circumstances.

Is there an entity with every person who is having an operation?

We are all connected with each other and during an operation we enter into an even closer connection with you. This connection is maintained as long as the process of healing has not been completed. It is only afterwards that this connection relaxes into a normal connection.

That means that you are then still with us?

Yes, exactly.

Are you a kind of angel?

You do not need to make a comparison. It is what it is.

Okay, dear entities. You are different from those that have names, right?

Yes. Those beings are the chosen ones who can make direct contact with the human beings. We stay behind them.

So you are like a legion of helpers behind them, is that right?

Yes.

And you are legion?

Yes.

From which level are you?

We are from the level of the protective energies.

Can you tell me whereabouts this is?

The fourth level, but we dwell in several different levels. Most beings start to perceive us from the second level upwards.

Have you ever been incarnated in human bodies?

No.

How can we visualize you?

You can visualize us like white energy in the shape of an orb.

And you move as an orb?

Yes.

53

Approximately how big are you? (They are sending me an image of a pilgrim carrying a gourd but since this image is not really contemporary, I ask again) Are you the size of a foot ball?

Yes. Here in Abadiânia we appear in this form as a rule but we are able to change it at will.

What does this depend on?

It depends on the willingness of the person asking for cleansing. The willingness to open up and the devotion to the task.

I understand. Where do you come from? Did you come here at one point or have you always been here?

We have been here when there were no other beings here. This place is our home on earth.

What is it like for you, when you give so much love and then at a given time you cannot help, isn't it terrible to be so powerless?

It is. This is why we do not wish to talk about this any further. Love is not a power you demand to have back. You give it freely.

Do you communicate with each other?

Yes, imagine us as a separate people. We are genderless and we multiply through division.

54

How does this happen?

Through intent. This division is irreversible.

Is this a kind of sister or twin energy?

It is a kind of twin energy.

Isn't it strange to be multiplied a thousand times?

No. This is a human type of judgment.

I understand. Can you explain again… You are of the fourth level, but you can operate here, right?

Yes.

Okay. Is this place representative for the fourth level?

This place is very connected to the love energy of the fourth level.

As you do not have an organism of the kind we are familiar with, you do not need to eat. How do you nourish yourselves?

The energy fields take nourishment from certain energy sources.

For instance?

We take nourishment from the sun.

The sun? A physical energy?

The sun is not only physical but also spiritual.

And are there such sources here on earth? How do you obtain the sun's energy? Do you just bask in the sun to absorb the energy?

Yes.

That is just like eating light.

Yes, exactly.

And how often do you need this nourishment?

All the time, the sun touches us. The sun is eternal and we receive its nourishment every second if you wish to look at it in terms of time.

Dear cleansing entities, what would you like to share with the people who will read what I am learning now?

The human beings need to learn to understand that their energy will never diminish but that the potential of their energy can change.

Can a human being during the course of his life reach the highest potential that is possible to a human in the cosmos?

Yes.

How?

Through cleansing.

You mean, through any form of spiritual cleansing? So the humans have the responsibility to transmute their energy?

Humans have the responsibility of being the creator of their own destiny.

So a human can choose to walk a different path from the one he has been walking so far, whenever he chooses?

Yes. That is the gift of being human.

∞

Is there something that makes you sad?

Humans who do not decide to walk the path of healing.

And what makes you happy?

Humans we have healed.

Are you in close contact with Dom Ignacio?

Yes. He is very busy with his own task.

Does he know that you are here?

Yes.

Have you got another message apart from the one you have just given?

Humans do not live love enough.

Do you know why this is so?

The beliefs of your religions hamper the opening of the hearts.

When you are doing a healing... I mean when you heal the soul's energy, isn't this "just" an opening of the heart?

No. The heart is the portal through which the energy can enter, but we transform the energy, not the heart.

I would like to know from a statistical point of view… in the time that you have been active here, has the energy of the humans who came here changed significantly?

Human energy has become especially powerful in its negativity. We observe that the humans are falling into darkness more and more.

And this in the year 2013 where an elevation of energy is said to have taken place. Can you tell me more about this, what about this elevated energy?

The energy has been elevated but the humans are not participating.

58   What is the main reason for this? When you say that they do not live their love, it is a matter of the heart, isn't it?

Humans love only their ego but they are not connected with the other worlds.

Thank you. Very well, I thank you.

Thank you for your willingness to convey messages to the world.

You are welcome.

∝

Dr. Valdivino

It is not known who he was on earth. He is a friendly, kind spirit; he deals with family matters and is very considerate toward everyone he treats. According to medium Joao, he once was a criminal judge.

(Source: Spiritual Healing, Ismar E. Garcia)

Interview

I now have the very great pleasure and honour to call on the entity that appears to us humans in the guise of Dr. Valdivino.

Dr. Valdivino, your energy feels so unbelievably soft that I have the urge to cry. Why does it feel like this?

> *The energy that I am feels like love to you. I love very strongly. It allows me to understand humans in their desperation. A perception that I also have been living in my lifetime.*

Dr. Valdivino, I read that you were a criminal judge once. Is this correct?

> *For a time, but not for long. I was unable to support the rules of politics and justice for very long. I had been obliged to judge differently from what I felt in a large number of cases.*

Then let us take a deeper look into your story. Please begin where you wish and tell us about it.

> *I have travelled to many countries as a child because my parents had to observe their political affiliations. I was always with them. The time alone when they were abroad again and I could not go with them was my favourite time.*

So you like to be alone, right?

> *I wouldn't say that, I liked to be undisturbed, left in peace, not trav-*

elling, but I had to travel a lot.

How did your life continue?

My parents indicated to me that I was to be a judge but I never wanted that. It was the quality of that time to be in need of judges.

Did you have a heightened perception for spiritual matters? Can you even remember things like that?

No.

But you felt an increasing divergence between the laws of human society and your intuition?

61

Yes. The rules were too inflexible for me and they disregarded the interconnection between people. We judged people like cattle on the market.

What happened then, what did you do then?

I could no longer support this type of judgment and I needed to find a new pattern for my life, so I gradually dissolved my connections to these matters and started on the path to freedom.

Where did you go then?

The first station on the way was a church.

What did you learn there?

There, I started to pray for guidance, to be shown the way to the liberation of my soul. The Virgin Mary appeared before me and told me what to do.

How did you perceive her?

I heard her.

And how did you know that it was she?

An internal voice told me that it was she.

Did you hear her again in your life?

Seldom.

What exactly did she tell you?

That I should make a pilgrimage to the holy sites of Mary around the world because that way, I would meet the people and experience the healing that I was seeking. I did that and started travelling the world.

Did you have an experience that touched you?

This experience touched me.

So you travelled a lot – and how exactly did your life continue?

I travelled far in order to find the answers that were inside me and I found them.

Would you like to tell me what those answers were?

Yes, I would love to.

Please tell me about your insights.

The first insight I had was that I am not alone, even when I am by myself. That made travelling a lot easier.

How did you come to this conclusion?

I understood that there are worlds within worlds and that we are all interconnected. Then I had a vision during meditation that I was part of the energy that is Mary.

How did you come to understand this during your meditation?

I understood how Her energy operates in the world. It is the female energy, and I began to experience its power.

Did you experience other energies as well or only the energy of Mary?

That was not important to me.

What was your next insight?

The next insight was that I was full of impurities and that the

cleansing should begin soon.

How did you realise that?

In a vision, during which I saw the soul as contaminated energy.

Can you give a brief example of how this contamination was shown?

The soul did not have a colour but I saw its energy as blue and there were dark spots in this blue. I wanted to get rid of these spots.

Did you also learn how to do this?

No; that was the task.

What did you do in order to cleanse yourself?

The gradual letting go of materialism was a first step towards letting go. Then I had to pray a lot, and I asked for forgiveness a lot and I forgave a lot. These two energies are very beneficial.

Was there a rhythm to this? How often did you do this?

I have tried to maintain a permanent state of prayer but I did not always succeed. But it was enough to cleanse me.

What was your third insight?

The third insight was that I was going to exist in perpetuity and not disappear after my death.

How did you arrive at this insight?

I had a vision in which I perceived the soul as a stage of a journey, where a life was a kind of cocoon like that of a butterfly. This perception made me understand the transmutation of energies that we experience here at every moment.

What was the fourth insight?

The next insight was that I could try and help with love, because every time I approached people with love, their alignment changed into a different direction... especially when those were angry energies, I could use the love that was inside me to change their energy into something soft and warm. The people who experienced that were often so deeply touched that they wept.

65

Was there another insight?

The fifth insight was not to expect love in return. You give because you want to give but not because you expect something in return for this.

How did you arrive at this insight?

I needed it in order to understand that this energy is eternal but I did eventually understand it and then lived it.

And what was the next insight?

That was the realization that I could transform certain areas in a

very short space of time but not when transformation was not welcome! Free will takes precedence over all processes. These were my insights and I live them to this day – now in my new form.

Were there other encounters with people in your life that touched you beside the encounter with Mary?

Yes, many... I have never experienced encounters with people as neutral, always as an encounter with a brother or a sister. This was helpful in order to distance myself from the feeling of loneliness. The human family is very large when you perceive it.

But Dr. Valdivino, humans are not always nice, and it hurts even more when family members hurt you...

I quickly understood the problems of the people I met and I gave them tips about how to solve them. This made enemies into friends.

And the people accepted this just like that?

At that time it was like that, yes; I was allowed to experience it like that.

Did you have a wife?

Yes, but I had to leave her too, on my path to freedom. But I was always connected with her, I know that and I know that her energy did not suffer greatly.

Did you have children?

No, my child died at birth.

How did you cope with that?

I was very sad but I did not want to lose the connection that I had just started to sense and so I tried not to let the sadness get to me too much.

And then you went on a long pilgrimage?

Yes, that is the right term.

And what happened then?

One night, the soul was ready to transition by leaving the body. I was old and tired of travelling and I wanted to love without suffering. So I began to sever the connection to the body.

Were you alone?

Yes.

And then?

This transition was very interesting because I perceived the energy of the level of the Ascended Masters and I was not sure who they were but I tried to make contact with them.

When you left your body, was there a transitional state?

Yes, the perception was a little foggy at first but in a relatively short period of time I perceived the beings behind the fog.

How did you perceive them?

The energy of these beings was very powerful and bright. I felt very happy there. Feeling this energy. Then I began to understand that I had died.

Were you able to communicate with these beings immediately?

Well, it took some time but I began to understand them shortly after. But this understanding is different from the one that you know; it starts with a feeling.

How did it happen that you found Joao?

With the masters, there is a perception you can begin to experience if you wish to help. I wanted to help; to love. And since I did not want to stay on the spiritual level only but on the other hand did not want to incarnate, I found my destiny in this task. Then I introduced myself to Joao by bringing my presence to him. He perceived it and gave permission to enter him. I like doing this because it allows me to experience human contact and to live the love that I really feel.

Then let us have a look at Abadiânia now. When you are inside Joao – how do you perceive the human beings?

∝

*I recognize their sadness and their pain and I can communicate to
them how to overcome them.*

Do you want to give the people a message?

**Yes, with pleasure. I feel how they lose themselves in sadness
and helplessness but I want to tell them that you are never alone.
Never! The power is crucial in order to feel connected. Therefore you should try to seek out empowering and not disempower-
ing moments.**

What are the most crucial mistakes on the path to healing?

People do not trust enough.

But in our world, trust can only be established by adhering to a framework. But you always insist how important it is that we liberate ourselves from the confinement of a too narrowly defined framework. How
does this fit together?

*This is true but you must distinguish between trusting the form and
trusting the cosmos.*

What do you think of the church as an institution?

*I hold this form in esteem but I am confused about how they misuse
this chance to liberate the people and achieve the exact opposite. I
would like to establish a new church if I could, but I cannot and I
do not want to come back in order to do this.*

But the people need beliefs and religion, what would you suggest?

I would suggest that they sharpen their perception within this framework so that every time there are limits they can overcome them instead of accepting them as limitations. Love is limitless!

How did you get the epithet of "Dr."?

The humans gave me that.

Are you happy, Dr. Valdivino?

Yes.

When did you perceive Dom Ignacio for the first time?

That was on the level of the Ascended Masters. There, he became a friend to me very quickly because I really liked his way of sharing perception and we communicate a lot. This communication is a great help to me in order to stay optimistic.

Why "optimistic"?

Because the people are losing connection. They believe that prayer and confession will liberate them but I must caution them that prayer and confession are not the only keys to purification but that the cleansing takes places inside of us.

Dr. Valdivino, please do not be sad. Please regard this book as another step towards helping these empty shells to fill with more awareness.

∞

These words are helping me a great deal because sometimes I do not believe that our work here is really understood.

Please let me focus on that particular point now. If you perceive that people are led by empty shells, what would your counsel be in order to lead them away from it?

It is wonderful that you let me answer these questions. The people should come here with the awareness that we are the chance that allows their soul to undergo transformation. Silence is an important key to this. These group travels are not good.

But I was grateful that I could travel in a group when I first came here. Do you have any comments on that?

That the people should read these lines and absorb them into their innermost knowledge about the connection. And then they should travel alone if they could. People who need help should of course travel with assistance, but generally it is more important that people be more quiet. Any communication between each other only serves as a distraction. Silence is the signpost and here, silence is the portal to the soul! The loud words in the hall in order to entertain the people are not helpful. I do support the prayer but I do not support the talk of those people who strive to entertain the travellers. The people should concentrate on themselves and go into silence in order to prepare themselves to come before Joao and the energy of the entities. This preparation will begin in the hall, and when this preparation is not allowed to take place in silence, it is like a lost pilgrimage when they come before Joao.
The people need love.

And what can we tell them about where to find it?

They find love in themselves. Love only needs our inner silence in order to grow. The distractions of your world and the fearful thoughts of the people around you will diminish this love. Therefore it is important that you rest and feel in harmony with the entities instead of feeling in connection with the attention-seeking tools of your time. Silence is the tool of your soul.

Many are afraid to look into silence, because people are afraid to be alone.

I can understand that, but this is just a phase that will pass as they enter into the next phase.

72 Are you a happy or a sad entity?

I am a very sad entity because I can feel the peoples' sadness and pain.

Was this the reason I felt the urge to weep?

Yes, but you also had to weep because you felt the love that is in me and you cannot separate the two.

Is there a place that you can suggest that people go, a place where they can find silence?

The place is not important.

Would you like to suggest a place in Abadiâna?

This place is a permanent call to enter into silence so it is impossible for me to point out a single place.

Would you like to add anything to that?

I have already talked a lot about my perceptions but I can tell you more about my way of communicating.
I perceive the people's sadness as disconnected energy.
This energy is like a harness. This harness needs love energy in order to be dissolved and that only happens little by little. Therefore, I can but ask every person to go into the energy of love and to open up in order to dissolve this harness.

How many people who come before you want healing and how many are there who only want attention?

73

This is an important question. I can tell you that most people only want attention when they are ill, because illness brings them attention.

And we tell these people that they should not seek love in this way but in themselves.

Yes, exactly, this attention that they are seeking through this means is not the attention that we call love energy. It is a contamination of the soul's perception and only serves to confuse the soul who is seeking help; because the soul seeks transformation but the human being seeks attention. You also call this ego.

∞

When the people realise that the love they seek is within them and cannot come from outside of them, they can start on the path to true destiny and fulfilment as part of love. But this experience will only be open to them if they place love above the ego's attention seeking. The experience of happiness cannot be found outside but exclusively as a result of the experience of love INSIDE YOU.

Can you tell me whether the number of these people has stayed the same or has increased?

This fact has been a constant over many years. The number of attention seekers and the number of those who really desire healing has always been the same.

But the problem is that many people really believe that they seek healing and are completely unaware of the fact that all they really seek is attention! How can we make them see that this is a false perception?

That is easy to perceive. They find attention through excessive communication with other people about this illness. Those who come here and who say little about this but listen in silence are the people who really seek healing.

Dear Dr. Valdivino, what exactly happens when you work with this tool/ pair of pliers in the nose of a patient?

The energy we use when this happens is like an injection into the soul. We inject the power we possess into the body and through this into the soul. This is because we have to make use of the openings that are there. You already know that the people have to be open in order to receive energy.

Yes, I know that. But why don't you use the mouth?

This is not possible because there are organs that swallow and block the passage. Therefore we need another opening that is large enough to receive the power without blocking its passage.

I see, and the passage via the eyes and ears is too narrow, right?

Yes, exactly.

Isn't there a danger of hurting people?

No, this action is located so deep down in the body that the power goes directly into the soul without hurting the body. This is like a needle that only scratches the surface but still reaches the surface. You can imagine this like an accelerating energy that is directed into the layers of the person by this tool. This is the special thing about this method; it is very violent. People who are subjected to this type of treatment are very closed off.

Could you say that here, the transfer of energy cannot happen by touch alone but that it needs something as violent as this?

Yes and no. This is not about the perception of the power that we convey but about the openness of the person. This is a type of operation that we use on people who are full of doubt within themselves.

And the white orbs are watching over this in order to make sure that nothing goes wrong, correct?

Yes.

I once saw how someone started to bleed copiously after such an operation where normally there is no blood. What exactly was the reason for that?

Then his inner blockages were so strong that we had to use a lot of force, otherwise there would have been no result at all. The pathways were so crusted over that we had no other possibility. The blood is a sign for he energy flow that was re-established. We always keep a close eye on operations of this kind. Do not be alarmed.

Did I understand this correctly; you always use the same amount of energy (depending on what the person is able to tolerate in his soul) but you use this type of operation on people who doubt very much, in other words, are rather crusted over?

Yes, that is right.

And what is the quality of the operations on the eye?

There, as well, we are making use of an opening into the soul but it is a softer method where we do not have to inject the energy in to the soul by such violent measures; the blockages are not so strong.

Dear Dr. Valdivino, I thank you for this great and extensive conversation.

I am really very happy that you put these messages out into the world. It is important and necessary. I thank you.

77

Dr. Augusto de Almeida

"My phalanx comprises not of ten, nor a hundred but thousands of Helping Spirits. I am the one who reaches to the very depths of the abyss to save a soul."

Not much is known about him.

Dr Augusto de Almeida is one of the most frequent Entities at the Casa de Dom Ignácio. He is reported to have been in the military, a rubber tapper and a doctor in previous incarnations. When Dr Augusto incorporates he is recognized for his strong personality and his somewhat authoritarian manner. He is known to be extremely kind and is deeply loved by all. "My phalanx comprises not of ten, nor a hundred but thousands of Helping Spirits. I am the one who reaches to the very depths of the abyss to save a soul."

Frequent visitors of the Casa can usually pick him out easily by his energetic manner that demands a lot of discipline from those who participate in his work.

In his lifetime as a doctor he experienced much suffering and pain among his patients due to the fact that anaesthetics and painkillers were as yet unknown. Patients had to bite down on a piece of cloth to bear the pain while he was operating upon them. Because of all the pain he has had to witness, he now works in Dom Ignacio's Casa where he conducts healings and surgical operations as well as taking care of the alleviation of the patients' pain.

He has a strong sense of justice and conducts his work with the utmost seriousness, allowing no interruptions of his procedures.

(Source: Spiritual Healing, Ismar E. Garcia)
and: http://www.healingbrazil.info/entities.htm

Interview

Dear entity that is known as Dr. Augusto among humans, I am happy to make your acquaintance. I would now like to know a bit more about you. Is there something you want to mention first of all?

A lot.

Let us begin with your last life. Is that okay?

Yes.

Then let us start with your last life. What were the important stages in your life? Was there something special about your childhood or adolescence?

My childhood was very nice and I had a lot of people who supported me. Then I joined the military, wanting to study internal medicine. I did this and spent much time with this task.

Were there things that especially affected you while you were doing this?

There were many.

Tell me about them.

I spent most of that time dealing with the people's desperation resulting from their injuries. This took a lot of strength. But I was privileged to learn a lot during this work.

Did you also amputate legs and things like that?

Yes.

So you studied internal medicine and also worked as a surgeon?

In principle, the military is like a university.

Dr. Augusto, I am still looking for the bridge, the experience that moved you to become the entity that you are now. Please tell me what moved you during your life?

You have to help me to find the words. The sadness I felt in those days was much stronger than I am able to put into words.

I understand. What made you sad?

The futility. Being unable to alleviate the suffering.

Did you have wife and children?

Yes.

And were you interested in spiritual matters?

Yes, I was.

And how did you pursue them?

Through meditation and silence, I sought to find the answers to how to deal with my sadness. But I have also explored other matters through this.

Which matters for example?

The soul.

That is interesting. What exactly did you explore?

The soul energy.

And how did you do this?

I tried to categorize the human soul energy into categories of soul energy. This made it easier for me to understand why some people had more soul energy than others.

I can subscribe to that. I have also written a book on this subject. I have talked about 1000 Watt light bulbs… but that won't mean anything to you now because you did not have electricity then, isn't that right?

Yes, it does make sense. The strength of a soul is linked to its awareness.

Yes, I agree. And then you were an explorer of the soul, just as I like to be now. Did you have more insights then?

The soul is never separated from the source. But humans are not consciously aware of this all-connecting energy.

∞

How were you able to measure this or how did you come to this conclusion?

*Through the worried, unloving energy that people emanated I came
to know that they were not consciously connected.*

Did you meet people with high awareness during your lifetime?

No, not many times.

What happened then? Did you have other insights?

Yes.

For instance?

That the people are not very aware of their I-AM presence.

You mean that they do not live in the moment, right?

Yes.

Any further insights?

*Further insights were that I could not make people become enlight-
ened if they did not want to be.*

Yes, I can understand that. Did you have these insights when you were
in the military or how did that happen?

I had these insights during that time and many of them afterwards.

For instance?

The nature of the soul is a malleable shape.

What exactly do you mean by that?

The soul energy is like a ball of rubber.

Caoutchouk.

Yes. That is right.

84 Like a caoutchouk energy?

Yes.

Go on…!

You can influence the shape of this energy. I noticed that when I was treating people while thinking of something beautiful. Then they were changed by these thoughts.

How did you perceive this transformation?

Through the joy that slowly took shape inside them, without me having used any words.

That is beautiful. It seems that you have conducted veritable experiments on the soul during your lifetime.

Hm.

And have you been working as a doctor all the time during that lifetime?

Most of the time.

And then?

Then I enhanced my time though travelling.

You travelled with wife and children?

Yes.

One child?

Two. A boy and a girl.

Dr. Augusto, what was your transition like?

I would like to keep that information to myself.

No problem. But can I ask how it happened that you came to work here after your passing? What were the components of this decision?

That is a long story. I began to experience more of the joy on the

other levels. This made me understand that love is an agent of heal-
ing that I had been unable to employ during my lifetime. But this
special power was more easily accessible to me on the spiritual
plane than in the human body. So a wish was growing inside me to
be able to help humans through this love.

And how did you get to Abadiânia and to Joao?

Then I started to look around for an energy that was pure enough
to work with. I found it here in Abadiânia.

Okay, and then?

Then I saw how Joao works in this function and I began to work
with him.

Dr. Augusto, now I have a question. Did you introduce yourself to him
and he said, "come to me"?

Yes, that was about it.

Since then, you have been going there and you are conducting these operations together; on the visible and invisible plane. What can you tell
me about the visible, i.e., physical operation?

These operations are a very connecting activity.

What do you mean by that?

The type of operation is a connection; we are strengthening the con-

nection though this process.

I don't really understand this very well. Please can you choose different words? With connection, do you mean the connection to Joao or to you?

> *The people who have this operation in their body are being brought into a state of utter devotion. This devotion is the key.*

What, the devotion?

> *Yes.*

Then you have to explain to me how this operation is necessary when all you really need is the devotion. Wouldn't it be enough to just touch their skin so that they feel something; anything?

> *In principle, this would be sufficient, but I know that people think in visual terms and so I prefer to construct visible connections through visible operations for their benefit.*

Sometimes you scratch the eyes. What exactly happens there?

> *Then we go into the part of the soul that is connected with the eye. It is like working on a meridian.*

But then why don't you work on meridians?

> *Please be careful with your questions, this can serve to confuse the people.*

Oh, sorry. All right, so you choose the eyes because through them, you are able to reach the meridian on which you wish to work. What exactly happens while you scrape around in there?

The meridian soul energy that flows in there is being cleansed.

Dear Dr. Augusto, when you perform other operations on the body... sometimes you make cuts and such things, but there is never really any blood... or very seldom at any rate. Can you give an explanation for this? How do you do this?

This is very easy. We anaesthetise this place.

How do you do this?

We treat this place with energy so that hardly any blood will flow and then the perception of this place will change. This means less sensitivity on the one hand and less blood on the other hand.

When you say you anaesthetise these places, how do you do this?

This happens through a special kind of energy that we receive from the healing entities.

How can I imagine this? Can you paint a mental picture for me that I can pass on to the people? When you are incorporated in Joao for instance and he uses the tools around him... When do the shining orbs work on the people? I may call the healing entities shining orbs, can't I?

Yes.

∞

When do these orbs works and how?

These shining orbs prepare the operation very quickly. In your terms, this happens within a fraction of a second. This information needed by the place of the operation will be initiated into it like an injection into the person's aura. There, it is active for a short period.

That means, when Joao begins to call people to the stage...

Yes.

Most of the time, he places them along the wall or he asks them to sit down.

The orbs begin their work as soon as the decision has been made.

89

Okay. Then you start to work and then the people will be asked to lie down in the room next door. What happens there?

There, the information will be removed from the aura and the healing process can resume. This process is subject to the person's own responsibility but we accelerate this process through the operation.

Okay, do you want to tell me something about these visible operations? Something you want to share with the people so that they may know... so that they can follow this advice?

I would be happy to. The operations that people receive here are not comparable with those that you know in your world. The actual operation takes place in the soul. Soul energy is activated and this initiates the healing.

Dear Dr. Augusto, how do you feel on the level that you are now with your insights?

You can imagine how I feel. I am very relieved that there is a way to really heal the people.

Did you never want to come back to earth?

No. The way of existence that I am privileged to experience here is the best one for me. I am not trapped in a body and yet I can utilize a body in order to help. Add to this the relief that I will not die with this knowledge but that it will endure forever and I can be this way forever until I may wish to change that.

90

Dear Dr. Augusto, would you like to say something about the invisible operations?

The invisible operations will become more numerous in the future because it is very important to me that the people receive such operations.

Why is it so important for you?

This is a question of energy. The people are losing more and more energy through their way of losing connection. This loss is costing them a lot of power. This results in a vicious cycle. Less energy means less connection. Less connection will result in the loss of even more energy.

I went through an operation yesterday and I had a very interesting experience, in that I felt my energy, I felt that I was being cleansed, that things were removed. Can you corroborate that or how do you perceive these operations?

I can corroborate that. Your perception is very exceptional and you will give the people a lot of valuable information through this perception, which could make the people more aware.

Dear Dr. Augusto, what would you like to tell the people when they are about to deliver themselves into your hands?

That they please should place more trust in energy entities...

Are you saying that you are the energy entities or that everyone is?

The entities that incorporate in Joao are the power entities. The others are the helpers.

And the helpers are also those that do the cleansing?

Hm... the cleansing is done by us and the cleansing entities support the process.

This morning I conducted an interview with a shining orb that called itself an entity of cleansing. I just want to place it correctly. So in the final analysis they are helpers, right?

∞

Yes, that is what they are.

They are a multitude. But if you do the cleansing and they are the entities of cleansing... why don't we call you entities of cleansing as well?

You could do that but we are a little more personal.

Hm, I understand, this is why you are not "just" entities of cleansing but also memories of your previous lives and the accompanying experiences inside an organism, right?

Yes.

Okay, that makes sense. Okay, Dr. Augusto, is there something that makes you sad?

The people's sadness makes me sad, because I cannot help, because I cannot always explain everything to them in order to take away their sadness.

And is there something that makes you joyful?

The connection of the energies; that is a wonderful, very pleasing feeling.

When a soul regains connection, right?

Yes.

Dear Dr. Augusto, you seem very strict, why is that?

Very strict?

Well, very serious.

This is a result of my last training as a military doctor. This was the way we communicated at that time, and that is still my way.

Do you think that you will lose this habit with time?

No.

I am only asking because people tell me about you, that you are always very strict during your operations and that you become very serious when people are not disciplined enough during this work. But, you know, joy is also important.

93

I know that. But this work requires a lot of attention on our side and we also need this attention from the people, and this is why I must bring them into shape.

I understand that. Have you got an opinion concerning human beliefs?

The people appear less and less connected. That is a great problem.

Do you have an idea how they can overcome this problem?

They can do this very easily by ceasing to look for answers on the

*outside but instead to look inside themselves. The language of the
soul is a language that does not need words.*

What is the most common mistake that people make?

*The people who come here usually remain in the consciousness that
they always had. But I wish that they would move on.*

You mean their consciousness should move on.

Yes.

I can confirm that but I still have not found the answer as to why they are
not doing this. Why do you think they do not choose to do this?

94

*I cannot answer this. I respect the free will and I protect the choice
but I cannot always understand them.*

One entity told me that it regrets the fact that people come here to get attention and not in order to really receive healing. Can you confirm that?

Yes... unfortunately.

Is there a place where you are? Are you here or on another level?

*I am on the fourth level, as are we all. I work from here; influencing
the world of matter. You are now connected with the fourth level.*

When you incorporate into Joao, how does this feel?

∞

It feels very constricted. You are so much smaller than the energy of our souls.

Earlier on in the crystal bed I had the perception of an entity with rather large hands taking my hands... is that about right in terms of dimensions?

Yes.

But then you must be at least twice as big as Joao.

Exactly.

Okay, and when you are in the rooms where the people meditate, where exactly are you then?

We are in the rooms that you visit but you must not confuse consciousness and form; we are mostly there in consciousness and not in our entire spiritual form.

Yes, I understand, that makes sense. How many entities are usually present in their entire form?

Mostly there is only one entity. The rest of us work from the fourth level.

Oh, but the white orbs are all there?

Yes. The orbs are the helpers.

∞

Could you say that the orbs are like angels?

Yes. (He laughs.)

It is nice that you do laugh once in a while.

But I do laugh.

Yes, but you seem to be so… strict.

I am sorry, but that is the way I am.

No, no, all is well. Would you like to say something else?

I regret that I am not as jolly as you would like me to be, but I am still connected with the impressions and experiences of my last life and that is why it is the way it is…

But that is perfectly okay. You do not have to apologize for that. I just wanted to tell you because I do not know if you are aware of this…

I know that.

Okay. Would you like to describe how you perceive the people when you treat them? I mean when you are inside of Joao…

I perceive their aura and the energy fields within them. Most of it is contaminated and it must be cleansed. And I can direct the people and tell them what they must do in order to experience their healing…

I am not sure, but can it be that I met you the first time I came here?

Yes.

And you said that you could heal me?

Yes.

What did you see?

That you still had a few contaminated fields inside you... But I know that you will have cleansed them soon and then your eyes will also improve!

Why is that? Just a moment, I am beginning to understand... When you use the eyes as a channel, a meridian of the soul, then my eyes are the indicator for the contamination?

Yes.

That is very exciting. Why doesn't anyone here tell me that?! I am sorry!

That's okay, I am happy to be here to answer our questions.

Okay, cool. So how do you perceive a strong connection?

I do that by seeing that the soul is connected upwards into the energy of the cosmos...

How can I imagine this cosmic energy? Does it extend a ray or a rope? What is it like?

You have to imagine this like a connecting line reaching out into the cosmos.

Ah, okay. And when you say that the people are not connected... I don't believe that the line ever breaks, but what does this connection look like in such a case?

It is very fine and thin.

Ah. And when you are fully connected, it is thicker?

Yes.

And how do you recognize that people, like myself, have a gift? That a gift develops...

We recognize this by the shape of the line. The line is very thick then.

Ah. So when you told me that I am developing a gift, the line was already very thick?

It was and it is. This is how you access the information that the cosmos has in store for you and this channel is your gift.

And how will this channel and myself change over time? Here, through this purification... will this make the channel even wider, will it change colour; how am I to visualize this?

The colour of the channel will turn whiter.

Oh, that is nice.

That is not "nice". That is the reality.

Dear Dr. Augusto, are there many people with a wide channel like that?

No.

That is too bad really, but why?

I cannot answer that. It is as it is.

99

What is the usual type of connection of the people who come here?

Most people's lines are slightly deformed and do not appear too strongly connected. I am trying to strengthen this connection through the meditations there, but it is a very arduous task. The people's thoughts are the problem. Their fears and blockages constantly jeopardize the process. I am really quite speechless sometimes as to how slowly these processes unroll because it really is not that complicated. But sometimes the people block their own development.

Yes. Do you have an explanation for why they are doing this?

I cannot tell you, I do not know.

Was there ever a healing session that really affected you?

No.

Hm. Is this because you generally do not perceive a lot about the humans?

It is so because we concentrate on staying in our energy; therefore we cannot concentrate on the people and their issues. This is what the people have to do themselves.

Yes, I understand. I do not remember whether it was Dom Ignacio who said it or one of the other entities... they explained that it was a sort of firing-up of energies that you are doing.

Yes. The soul receives energy; that is the key. This energy can move the soul... into its own healing, or the people can block this healing again. That is no longer my task.

Is there an entity you are in contact with very often?

That would be the entity of Dr. Valdivino.

What do you like about him?

The love in him is very great. He is like a father to me.

Is there such a thing as a feeling of loneliness where you are?

∞

Very seldom, but I know what you mean. It is not loneliness you feel over here. It is the isolation of a task, but I am afraid those are not the right words. Because isolation is not the right word either. Nothing is separated and we do not feel separated here. This is why isolation is not real. What I mean is that the concentration on this task really requires a lot of attention. This energy then becomes unavailable for other things in the cosmos.

I understand... but it is what it is.

Exactly.

Dear Dr. Augusto, what message do you want to give to the people?

That they should be more trustful. Healing is not a thing that can be attained over night, but it is a path and you need to take many steps to walk this path. So please convey to them that they should be patient because energies do not change over night. This is a process.

101

Do you have a favourite place here in the *Casa*, a place where your consciousness especially likes to dwell in?

That would be the chapel.

You all like to be in the chapel – why?

The energy there is very high and very pure. I like this place very much.

∞

What can I do in the chapel?

That is up to you. The chapel is just a place that is especially pure.

Wonderful. Why is that?

I cannot answer that.

Dear Dr. Augusto, what else would you like to tell me?

That we are connected to the other parts of the cosmos. And this is why it is so much easier for you to communicate with us.

Can you tell me how you visually perceive *Abadiânia* or, let's say, the *Casa* and the space around it?

I would be happy to. I perceive this space as very white and full of light. I really do need another word for this but I cannot think of it.

I understand. Dear Dr. Augusto, what else do you want to say?

I would love to tell you how I felt when I treated the first person as an entity.

With pleasure.

At that time, I still was very, very much involved with the perception of my last lifetime, but I did try to concentrate and to perceive the energy of the person. Then I saw him and his energy fields. Then I knew that I was in the right place and I was very happy to finally have found a way to perceive the soul and to heal.

I can understand that very well. Oh, Dr, Augusto, my hand is starting to hurt. I believe we have to take a break. Can we continue later? What do you say?

That would be great.

You are really chatting away now!

I herewith charge you with contacting me again.

Oh, then I will do as you say, if you charge me with it.

103

This was a joke.

Oh, you are really funny.

That is nice, that I can make you laugh.

I am pleased. I will go and have something to eat now.

*

After my meal, we continue. I report back for recording.

Reporting back, "Colonel" Augusto. I am ready to record further information you wish to convey.

∞

I am pleased. I would like to tell you how the energy of a place is connected to the energy of the souls.

Yes please, that is very interesting. And it fits in really well.

The energy of a place is the reason why certain qualities incarnate there. This is similar to colours where certain colours enhance each other or appear disharmonious. The energy of a place always resonates with the energy of the people who dwell there.

That means – this is very interesting – is the energy of the place the cause for the local energy or is it the souls' energy?

The cause is the energy that is possible in this place but everything is always connected. Still the local energy is stronger. The place attracts the souls, or not, as the case may be.

104

I am currently living in Austria. Where would you place Austria energetically?

This land is very beautiful but the energy of the people there is a little constricting. The reason for this is your country's past history. I have visited Austria once as a human being and I was very much taken by the beauty of the mountains. But I felt how the people there are trapped in unconsciousness.

And what about Germany? Can you tell me something about the energy there?

That is similar. I have also been to Germany. It was the same thing there. The energy of the people there is very constrictive.

What about England?

England is better. Many cleansing entities have their place of power there. That is the reason why you find messages there that have been written on the fields. They come from the healing entities that would like to contact you so that you may awaken.

And what about France?

That is different from the other countries because this is the location of the energy line of destiny.

What is that?

105

The energy line of destiny determines the development of humanity in some regard. This energy line is like one of the earth's meridians. This is the energy line of the heart chakra. This connects with the heart energy of the people and this will show their destiny.

I understand. And what is the heart line telling us at this moment?

The heart line is telling us that the people are less and less connected with each other and that this allows the energy of humanity to wane. I am looking into this direction a little wistfully because I do not like to see what I see.

To be honest, I am a little speechless now because right now, humanity is boasting about being so intelligent, well developed and oh so interconnected... There are many charitable institutions, charitable funds and so forth... many institutions that help. How does this fit with the information that you have just given me?

Many people do not help out of love but out of calculation. This is the problem. This way, the act of helping becomes a mask like the Totem mask of the Indians.

And what is the cause? Can you tell me?

No.

This is dreadful. Sad, I mean. Very sad.

I cannot bear to look.

106

How can I picture this? Will the heart line diminish more and more?

Yes.

But that is unbelievable. That is really disillusioning.

It is, but we all hope that he people will become more vigilant and that impulses like yours will bring new movement.

Yes, I can understand that you do not want to watch. This siphons off energy, you do not want to face it... Let us continue. France is not longer as strong as it was energetically because the heart line is diminishing, right?

∞

Yes.

What about Italy?

The heart line is there as well but in another shape. The energies that converge in Rome are another matter altogether.

Oh, I am listening.

This is the crossing of the lines of the heart and of the belly. These two lines intersect in the middle, at the palace that you call "Dom".

St. Peter's Cathedral ?

That is the intersection.

107

Heart and belly?

Yes.

Belly? Isn't there a better term for this? The heart is an organ but the belly is not.

I do not mean the organ named heart. I mean the heart energy that flows there and the energy that flows in the belly. This is like the energy of motherhood.

What is the energy of motherliness good for?

The energy of motherhood creates things through the female energy.

So this is the convergence of heart and mother energy, in other words the heart line and the female line?

That is correct.

And why are there only men in this of all places?

Your question is the answer. The power potential of these two lines is so great that the people made an even greater effort to fight it there. This is why you will find no femininity over there at all.

What do you think about that from your perspective? After all, you have had dealings with the church yourself.

I find it very sad, that the people are so hungry for power. This power that is sent into the world in disharmony is the source of much suffering on this planet.

Okay, once more to make sure I understood: We have the heart line and the female line that intersect there… and right on top of this there is a building that only supports male energy. What exactly is the effect of only men living there?

These men who work and act there transform the female energy into male energy and by doing that, rob themselves as well as humankind of the power of the female energy.

I understand. According to you, is there anything that is good in the church? I mean, you did experience it as a human being.

The church is basically the embodiment of the "devil", as you like to call it. The Word "devil" signifies the negation of human feeling. Negation of love, but basically a form of love, just not in a shape that humans recognize.

Dr. Augusto, it is very nice to chat with you and I understand you very well. Talking to you is pleasant and smooth.

That is because you are already much more purified and because the energy here is more pure. Both components make for a smooth flow.

Great. What would you like to tell me about next, seeing that you are so happy to chat?

I want to tell you what we are doing with people who do not wish to be healed yet.

Yes please, I am listening.

These people are brought into a state of trance, during which they have the chance to let their soul speak. The language of the soul is not bound to words...

I know... when do you do that? When does this happen?

It depends. Sometimes it is during dreams, sometimes during medi-

∞

tations. We send them the energy that makes them drowsy and then the soul can begin to communicate.

So this is also part of the process over here?

Yes.

How do you recognize that a person does not wish to be healed?

We see that in the way that he takes things in. When he is open, then he is ready. When he is closed up, he is not ready.

And how does "open" and "closed" look energetically?

Very simple: The aura is open when it radiates.

110

Okay. What else do you want to tell me about this?

That we leave the responsibility of the choice to them (the people).

How do you recognize very evil people?

I do not see whether they are evil or not. I perceive their energy. But I think I know what you mean. I observe that many people have a closed heart. This is an indicator for what you experience as evil.

I understand. Is the openness of a heart closely linked with awareness?

No. The heart is the gateway to the other world but neither the proof for nor the cause of awareness. Heart energy is an energy that sup-

ports awareness but it is not the energy alone.

Then what is the important thing?

The heart connection.

The heart helps to establish the connection?

Yes.

But then it is very much engaged in the process.

That is right but it is much more than that.

You need the will… what else is needed?

You need willingness, merit, permission, the power generally, potentials, the environment, the right person, the right places, the right perception…

I understand. When you look at people, can you see something about their last life?

Seldom. And it is not really necessary anyway.

Well, there are people who believe in Karma and things like that. Some believe that the things they experience have their causes in a previous life, which is why I ask…

This is true but it is not my area of expertise. I see what I see and I

do not ask why I see it.

I understand. Can you see the future?

Yes.

How does that work?

That is very easy. You see the energy of the now and change it through your own will or the willingness, the intent, goals... and it is this willingness that prepares the way...

What do you want to talk about next?

112

Your concentration is waning. I think it is best to stop now, otherwise it will be too much for you.

Thank you. I will go to sleep now and interview the others tomorrow.

That will be nice.

I have one more question: Somebody once said that during your lifetime you were with the freemasons, is that right?

That is very interesting. Who told you that?

I believe that was Dr. Valdivino.

That's right.

∞

You were with the freemasons?

Yes.

And what do you think of this club?

I have learned many useful things there and I have learned to appreciate many contacts there. I know that nowadays this order no longer has any potential function, like we had in those days. That is a shame because it really was very nice there.

Please do not be upset with Dr. Valdivino.

No. He did not just tell you for nothing. Maybe there was a reason for doing that for himself or for you.

113

Good, then I will go to sleep now and observe everything you told me.

That is well and I am looking forward to seeing you again.

And me. Thank you and good night.

*

Okay, Dr. Augusto.. Good morning in *Abadiânia*. I bet just a moment has passed for you, right?

That's right.

I hope I have enough concentration now to ask you a few more questions, to understand correctly, what you are saying and to generally listen if you want to share anything else.

It is looking good. Your energy is very high.

Dear Dr. Augusto, I have been thinking… yesterday, you explained to me that you work on the eyes as a soul meridian. I once read that eyes and hands are soul meridians. Is that what you mean?

Yes. The energy is connected to the hands and to the eyes.

Which means that in principle you could also works on the hands, right?

No, the hands need to maintain an uninterrupted connection so that you can maintain your internal energy. But the eyes remain in a different state while we do this.

My hands are always very hot. What does this mean by your definition?

That is your connection. It is very strong and you feel this.

If the hands get any hotter through this cleansing process, they would be smouldering…

I am sure they will not but I know what you mean. They will tell you when you are in connection.

Dear Dr. Augusto, there is one thing I did not really understand: As you do not just work on the eyes... when you work on the shoulders or on other places... then you 'only' do this in order to induce a state of trance in the person in order to let their soul speak?

No, the incisions into the body also serve to remove the dirt from the soul. This is as if you would remove the brown skin from an almond kernel.

In other words, like an unshelled nut.

That is about what I mean.

I understand.

These operations accelerate the person's energy and that is their chance for further development.

What do you do when people come to you and ask for specific blessings? What exactly does that mean? How does that look energetically?

The blessing is a connection that we establish.

How do you establish that?

The connection happens when we merge our energy with theirs and this is how the connection is established.

When one day this book is finished, I should have it blessed, shouldn't I?

No, not really, because we are in contact with you and can bestow the blessing anyway.

Does it always need a blessing when a channel is about to cleanse itself?

No, but the people like this custom.

Okay, then we will talk about this when the time comes. How do you do this, by the way, when people stand before you and ask, ask, ask... you really only see energy fields, right?

It is hard for me but I try to read their energy fields.

I understand. I have once witnessed someone asking whether his wife was the right woman for him. You have to forgive me, I am almost judgmental now, but I found it almost a bit petty to come to you with such a question ... when there are so many people every day that come to you for help... The question seemed inconsequential to me in this context.

That is insignificant in comparison to some questions we have to answer. The people have no concept of the work that we do.

I hope we can change that. So, Dr. Augusto, I believe I have asked all the questions that have accumulated inside me and if you like, you can talk a little more about yourself. Would you like that? It seems to me that you would, right?

The energy here is very good for the healing of the soul. You have experienced this already, but what I want to share with the

people is that they are responsible for their own soul. Ultimately every person's awareness determines the further development of their soul.

You are making a distinction here. I had thought that the people are the souls... therefore it is the soul who makes the decisions... but that is not right... it is the ego, correct?

Exactly. The people are the creators of their ego. This ego then becomes the devil in their suffering. They have to realise this; that the power is not outside of them but inside.

This word is rather strong; devil. I have called it animal. Animal would be okay too, right?

That is all right and it is ultimately the same thing. The devil has always been shown as an animal.

117

Yes, that's right. But these images were created by the church and we both agree upon our opinion of the things that this institution is currently doing.

That is right.

Then let us work with images that are not connected to this context, otherwise we might be moving in the wrong direction.

This is also true. I am grateful when you help me to find the right words. I have not often got the opportunity to communicate like this. This is why it is new to me and also quite hard.

That's okay. It is also my task in some respect to change the language... Why is it, Dr. Augusto, that I have to yawn all the time?

This is the opening of your body in order to receive the impulses. You will in time experience this opening in an easier manner, not solely in this form.

I have to take care when yawning that no one else is entering me in this way.

Yes, that is why a safeguard is important.

Yes, I know. Which makes me remember: Can you tell me, when a being enters me in the way that I have experienced once with a deceased person, what exactly is in it for them?

Those souls of the deceased are in a state of desperation. They are desperately looking for a channel into the other world. This is the reason why they come to you - to get to the other world.

But they already are in another world, at least in comparison to me.

No, they are in our world, but they are no longer visible through the sort of body that you can perceive.

Yes, that's right. You are very specific; I like that. When I work with the crystals, I send them power, in other words energy, when they contact me. Is that about the same thing?

That is about the same thing. When you do that, you accelerate their

∞

energy and that changes their frequency. This enables them to arrive at another awareness. That is all.

Yes, that is the way I saw it as well. It is a type of catalyst; a rocket to another level.

Exactly, and that is practically the same thing that we do here. The energy accelerates the souls and that changes their perception.

I understand. And do you perceive the souls of the deceased at all, where you work?

No, there are none there. The energy is too high. The energies that operate here are located on higher levels. That is the pleasant thing about it.

119

I can understand that. I have received the task to help the deceased in that way... so in some regard I am working in the same capacity as you... just with the deceased.

You have said that well. We cannot see this work but we know that you can do it.

Please, if you wish, you can continue to explain.

I am really impressed how you do that.

I believe that, you inquisitive soul. How do you perceive what I am doing?

∞

You are connected to me and therefore you receive my answers: like souls when they communicate with each other. But it is your gift to translate these impulses into words that you understand. This is fascinating.

Where do you think this transformation happens - in my brain or in my heart? I am still casting about for answers concerning this subject.

I do not know that. I am very interested in finding out about that.

And how are you going to find out about that?

I do not know this myself as yet.

I am very curious about what you will learn... I will ask you some time whether you have found out. Maybe it turns out that I will not need my hand anymore one day.

That may be. I do not know.

Do you want to tell me anything else?

No.

Then I will call upon another entity today. Do you know anybody who might be interested?

You must talk to the energy that you call Solomon.

Are you in contact with him?

Yes, we are in very intense contact. He is my teacher.

Oh, your teacher. Okay, is he from your level or from another?

He is from another level, from a higher level.

But he teaches you, so this is possible? He perceives you?

Yes, it is possible. He perceives me. I learn from him when he talks to me in the language of the soul.

So you also perceive him.

Yes.

Is there another you would like to recommend and who has not yet been mentioned in these notes?

Be aware and you will receive the impulses. That is the only thing...

Yes, okay, then I will be open for this. I thank you with all my heart for your attention and your devotion...The things you told me were unbelievably interesting. I am happy to have found a fellow explorer in you because I believe that I feel that you see things like me through the eyes of an explorer and seek to understand them. I am on the same path and I am trying to communicate this information to the people in a clearer way by contacting you. I am very happy to have met you. It was and it is a great honour for me.

∞

You have said this very kindly. I thank you very much for these sweet words. I will stay in contact with you and will soon report what I find out...

Thank you very much.

Francisco de Xavier

Francisco de Gassu y Javier was born in 1506 at Javier castle near the city of Pamplona in Spain. He came from a noble family that owned much land and had many titles. He grew up in material abundance, steeped in old traditions. His intelligence compelled him to study many different subjects. From the age of nine to the age of 29, Franciso attended the College Santa Barbara in Paris, where his room mate was Pedro Fabre. This friendship was very beneficial to his brilliant and impulsive nature. There, he also met Calvin who was to be a major figure in the Protestant revolution in Europe. It was also at the College Santa Barbara that he met his future mentor Ignacio de Loyola. They formed a close friendship and when Francisco's parents withdrew their financial support, it was Ignacio who stepped in to help.

He graduated in philosophy in 1526 and was made a professor in 1530. On August 15, 1534, together with Pedro Fabre and four friends, he made a vow to live in poverty and chastity under the guidance of Ignacio de Loyola. They were the first Jesuits, members of the Society of Jesus. Francisco went to India, Japan and other countries of the Orient to spread their philosophy.

He died on December 3, 1552 at 46 years of age on an island on the coast of China, having travelled more than 12000 kilometres during his lifetime. His coffin was filled with chalk in order to accelerate decomposition of the body, which would allow his friends to transport his bare bones back to Europe. But when the coffin was opened more than three months later, they were astounded to find the body in a perfect state of preservation with no smell of decomposition. The body was brought to

Malaga and then to the church of Bom Jesus in Goa, where it is an object of veneration to this day.

Francisco de Xavier performed many miraculous healings during his lifetime. Many miracles that happened through praying before his mortal remains are ascribed to him even now.

He wrote many wonderful letters, which Ignacio de Loyola copied out and distributed to be read in the churches as examples of an exceptional life.

Francisco de Xavier was canonized on March 12, 1622 and is regarded as the senior Apostle of modern times in the same vein as Saint Peter was the senior Apostle of ancient times. Considered the greatest of all missionaries, Pope Pius XI made him the patron saint of missions and missionaries.

124

(Source: Spiritual Healing, Ismar E. Garcia)

Interview

Dear entity that is known to the people as Francisco de Xavier, I am happy to be allowed to meet you and I ask you for an interview.

I am ready...

I would like to introduce myself as a human being who would like to communicate your message to her fellow human beings in order to allow them to enter the healing process here more consciously. Please tell me about your life and your work so far. Where are you now?

I am on the fourth level, where we all are.

Your energy feels very subtle and loving. Do I perceive this correctly?

Yes, that is right, I represent the most refined quality amongst the entities.

Dear Francisco de Xavier, please let us begin with your life. Would you like to tell me about the special moments in your life?

Meeting Ignacio was the most incisive encounter of my lifetime. I will never forget that moment.

What made this moment so special?

The love he radiated and the connection was new and fascinating to my entire being. The energy was very high. I felt deeply un-

∞

derstood by him and I wished to be like him. This compelled me to walk the new paths.

What did you do?

I abandoned my studies and entered into meditation. Through this, I comprehended many of Ignacio's perceptions and was later able to emulate this. That was important to me and I achieved that.

Were you ever married?

No.

Did you have children?

126

No.

Did you perceive the spiritual world?

I have always perceived the peoples' energy differently. It was like in a theatre, sometimes they were nice, then they were evil, then they were funny, then they were serious. I have never been able to under-stand the way of these humans. But I tried.

What compelled you to follow the path that you chose then and what exactly was this path?

The next steps were the instruction of other people. I travelled a lot in order to do this and I loved it...

I read that you went to Asia, is that right?

Yes, that is right.

And you founded India's first Jesuit order on Goa?

Yes, that is right.

What made you most happy on your travels?

To re-establish the peoples' connection with the spiritual world was very fulfilling to me.

Were you not also often disappointed when it did not succeed?

I was, but I did not want to be dissuaded from this path; it is like the fable of the children who still stumble and cry loudly about it. This point of view helped me to cope with this.

127

It is written that you died on an island in Asia. Is that right?

Yes.

And it is also written that you were very tired and lonely then. Is that right?

No, I rarely felt lonely; I was always deeply conscious of the fact that I am never alone and will never be alone. The perception of the spiritual energy is like a family.

∞

May I ask about your transition?

No. I would like to keep this experience to myself.

Would you like to tell me more about your life?

That it was filled with love.

Were you able to develop your abilities further during your lifetime?

I have in due time been able to better perceive the people's energy. I have consciously observed their bodies and was then able to perceive the personalities inside them. The many faces of a person are very revealing. A person's body is the mirror of his soul. The energy inside a body needs space, and the more refined the energy is, the more refined is the body. When the energy is rough and still contaminated, the body will be rough as well...

How do you explain people with strong physicality but very refined perception?

That is also possible but most people display this connection between spirituality and physicality. Only very few people are able to fully utilize material life and yet be very spiritual at the same time. That is very rare.

How can you recognize negative people?

That is easy to recognize. Look into the person's eyes. The eyes of a person show the strength of his heart. People with wide open eyes

and wide pupils are very open.

When a person has an eye disease, what can we infer from that?

You cannot infer anything from it. It only shows contamination of the soul. This must be removed but it does not have anything to do with the energy dynamics I was talking about. Love is located in the heart. The eyes serve as a channel leading into the heart. It is hard for me to describe but I have observed this for a long time. A person's energy needs time to establish its expression but the children carry the energy of their previous lifetime. That is very interesting because you can find a direct contact to their previous existence there.

But you cannot communicate with small children and therefore this information does not help very much. And by the time they can talk they are already too far away from this experience, right?

That is right, but it is an interesting fact.

Which people have touched your life besides Ignacio?

They were many because the way that I have approached them has changed a lot inside them, and it was a great gift to be able to observe this transformation.

Did you have a feeling then about whether or not you wanted to incarnate again?

I did not want to return because I knew that I had achieved all I

wanted to do and could do with my energy in that form, and I was worried about the shape that the new form might take.

Please tell me how you perceived the other world after your transition.

The other world is much more beautiful than I imagined. The only image in my head had been that of the angels because that is what we were taught, but I can tell you that there are many more wonderful beings here, especially on our level. This is very rewarding.

Which colour do you attribute to this level in your perception?

That is very variable. Different shades of white. The energies each have their inherent qualities, there are different tints of colour here and there, but basically it is all very bright here.

130

After your transition, how did you perceive Dom Ignacio?

The encounter was very joyful because I had hoped but not expected to meet him again so soon. It was really wonderful and I felt as if I had come home.

Did he then tell you about the way you are all working over here or what happened next?

Communication on this level works differently. You do not use words there but you feel the information. I felt Dom Ignacio's mission and I wanted to stay part of it, and this is why I also began to incorporate into Joao.

∞

Do you like doing that?

Yes.

What is your favourite part of working in the *Casa*?

I prefer to clean the souls through an operation; that is very connecting. You will remember that I have always loved to reconnect people.

How do you perceive the people that come before you when you are incorporated in Joao?

I read the energy fields in their aura. It assists in understanding the reasons for their illnesses. And then we embark on the path toward cleansing the energy fields. That is all.

131

And when there is an operation, you also perform it.

In some sense; yes. You know that we are not physically there; that we work from our level. We work with energy and we can do this most effectively when people consciously invoke us because then they are opening themselves to our connection.

Does this energy continue to flow from you to the people once you are connected to them?

Yes, it does.

And does this process drain you of power?

It does not do this because this is a circuit where we simply relay the power from the cosmos. We are the energy beings who are able to concentrate and utilize the power in order to accelerate the energy of the soul. That is our task.

What makes you unhappy about the people who come here?

That I cannot always help, because there are other problems in the cosmos where I am not permitted to interfere...

When does that happen?

When the soul has chosen its own path of healing and not our path. This has not been easy for me to understand but I have to accept it.

132

You mean that the process of healing is seeking its own path and not the path that you consider to be the right one.

Yes, exactly.

Are you happy, where you are now and with what you are doing now?

This form is the right one for me, this is my home and I do not wish to change this for a long time to come.

What are the operations like for you, how do you perceive them?

My teacher is Dr. Augusto. He shows me where and how I must cut if this is needed. And the many healing entities help me not to make a mistake.

You have experienced the Jesuit order and you were a companion of Dom Ignacio. The Society of Jesus still is part of the modern church. Has your perception of this church changed from then to now?

The church was our chance to bring our message into the world and we accepted that with mixed feelings, but I still think that this was the right step. The church still is the place that people come to in order to do good and to pray. This is a good starting point that we should use; but the way that the church is suppressing the soul is unforgivable. I see that differently now.

How do you perceive the power of the church today – from your point of view?

133

The church has been contaminated with power and ego and no longer has anything to do with the belief that we strove to impart. Nowadays it is as if you were hiring an actor to play the pope – the energy is that empty.

Did you ever have a close encounter with or a special connection to Jesus through the Society of Jesus?

No, this has not been my gift, but I still admire him.

Did you understand his message?

No, I did not. I was unable to see that he had been warning us, telling us to protect ourselves. The people who help are no better pro-

tected than other people just because they are helping. This is an important point because through this, the people who help are losing a lot of power and that is unnecessary.

What do you think was his warning?

The reason he went on to be crucified was not love for mankind but a warning, a call for love to protect itself.

You mean what he meant to tell us was something like "this is what happens if you do not protect yourself." Right?

Yes.

What is your take on the other religions of this world?

In Asia, belief is much more channelled. I have perceived the people's energy over there differently from over here in Europe. In any case, the people's ability to concentrate on themselves is more alive over there than over here. Here, the people do concentrate on themselves, but they are less connected.

What is your feeling about humanity at this point?

Humanity is going though a life-changing phase. This will need time but I am curious to see when they will make the leap.

How exactly do you perceive this?

I see the people's connection and I know what it produces is at cer-

tain times not very pleasant. I have to admit that. But when and how the people ultimately will find their way forward, that I am unable to perceive.

Is there something you are especially interested in – the soul or the body or the person?

I am less interested in the soul than in the person: I want to understand the connection. The decisions that people make are being formed much earlier than they perceive. This is very interesting to observe because I have not yet been able to find where exactly the crucial impulses are given, when a path goes into the wrong direction. I would like to be able to pre-empt that but I cannot.

What else would you like to tell me?

135

Love is the only thing that people seek and need in their lives. It is very important to me that you communicate the essence of this, my message, in this form. The people need only love and they will begin to heal very soon.

Yes, but where would they find this love?

Then tell them that it is inside them. The soul's connection to the other levels is the key; and the feeling that you constantly have to look elsewhere, outside of yourselves, it is the wrong path.

Would you modify Dom Ignacio's Exercises from your current perspective?

∞

That is not easy; I have always liked the idea of the Exercises and always propagated them, but there are a few details that I would change now. But I can imagine that Dom Ignacio would like to tell you about that himself.

Are you in contact with Dom Ignacio a lot?

Yes, we are in constant communication, you have to imagine this like feeling as one and the same being... there is no division into You and I but there are memories of I and You, that is what makes us individuals but ultimately we are all part of the whole.

Do you have a body over there?

Yes, with your human eyes you would perceive an oval column of light.

Do you have eyes?

No, I do not need them; perception is many times more multifaceted over here.

Can you see the future?

No, I can read the past.

Then I thank you for this interesting interview.

I thank you too; please stay in contact.

∞

Jose Pereidos

Jose Pereidos is another popular entity that regularly incorporates into the body of Joao de Deus. This entity takes a lot of time to talk to the visitors and so the queue of visitors is moving very slowly when he is incorporated.

Source: http://www.casaguidebrazil.org/geistige-aumlrzte.html

Interview

Dear entity that is known to the people as Jose Pereidos. I am happy to get to know you, too.

My pleasure. You are in connection to me.

Yes, I am.

This is unusual because normally, I can only sense the energy of the questioner and I am unable to move his hand.

The people do not know much about you. May I ask you a few questions about your life?

Yes.

Can you describe a few stations of your life? What was your childhood like?

I was a very loving child and experienced the people as very wicked. This has moved me in my adolescence to go on a journey to seek out loving people. That was not easy.

When did you live?

That was long ago, the people did not have those utilities that you have for transport. I was on the road all the time.

So you were on a pilgrimage?

Yes.

Where did you start?

I started in France and took to the path to Jerusalem.

Why Jerusalem of all places?

I wanted to look for the love that I did not encounter in the people.

What was it that struck you as so unloving?

The people were very unloving when talking to each other. I always experienced this as small wars. That hurt me very much and I could not bear it, so I had to flee.

What did you experience in Jerusalem?

I visited several people who all lived the belief of their religion, but I did not find the love I was seeking.

What did you do then?

Then I travelled to Tibet to seek out the love that I wanted to feel.

And did you find it?

To some degree... The people there live their connection with God in more harmony than in western cultures, but even there, I waited in vain for the love whose essence I sought.

What did you do on your search?

I went into monasteries and studied the teachings of the Buddha, but that did not fulfil me either. Then I departed to India in order to study the Vedas.

How did you study them?

The people there taught them to me. These teachings were very helpful in my search for love because I grew in my understanding as to where I could find the love I was searching for. I stayed there until the end of my path.

Were there any moments that touched you on this path?

The people were always very self-absorbed but never in connection with their true power. That was the hardest thing for me about being human, because I felt the love inside me, but I never found anyone who felt the same thing. Not even through the love for a woman.

Did you have wife and child?

No.

Did you never miss that?

No, the love for a woman is transitory but the love inside me is without time and space; I wanted to find a partner who felt in a similar way but I have not found that with women.

Would you like to talk about this encounter?

The man that I am talking about was not my partner in the sense that you mean; he was a true friend. This encounter made a lasting impression upon me because I knew that the love that I feel is not mine alone, I just had to find the right person, then I would not be the only one to feel this.

What was your task, what sort of work did you do?

I taught the things I had learned on my travels. This type of work gave me a lot of joy.

141

How did you live?

I lived in a house.

How were you able to pay for all your travels?

I have always been able to finance my travels through my work as a teacher. I passed on the knowledge that I gained.

Were you happy in your life?

Yes.

What was the most beautiful thing that you experienced in your lifetime?

Meeting my friend.

And what was the cruellest thing?

The wickedness of the people; how they treated each other.

Did you die in peace?

Yes.

Would you like to talk about your passing?

Yes.

Then I will be happy to listen to you.

When I died, I was very tired. I went to lie down and I knew that I would not wake up again in this world but in another. I sensed that, I went to lie down and sent word to my friend. Then the process of detachment began. I died in small steps. First I perceived the limbo world. There, it is foggy and dark in some regions. Then I perceived the next level, where it was already lighter and clearer. This level was full of other entities who where waiting for me. That was very joyful and I was very happy to be in wise company. These entities were the friends of the Wise Brotherhood.

Did you perceive other entities in limbo?

No.

Were you afraid?

No.

What happened when you reached the Wise Brotherhood?

The Brothers greeted me and protected me from feelings of loss. I had been a little sad about leaving my friend.

What happened then?

I spent much time with them if you want to talk about it in terms of time. But at some point I started to ask myself about my task in the cosmos and then I embarked on the search for an answer to this question. The Friends of the Brotherhood did not wish to answer this question because I had to find out for myself. The journey is the reward, as you know.

143

What did you experience then?

The first encounter I had then was with Dr. Valdivino. This encounter was very fulfilling. He explained to me in his loving way that there was a place on earth where people go to get help with special support from the spiritual world. That would be a possibility for me to attain my goal. Then Valdivino introduced me to Oswaldo and he took me to this place.

How did you perceive this place?

The energy of this place corresponded to the energy of the level of the Ascended Masters. Then Oswaldo began to show me how he brought the power of his being into Joao's body in order to be able to talk to the people. Joao's body extended inside and Oswaldo's energy was able to enter into him. The layers were wide and open. This enabled this process. Then the layer began to close a little and Joao's body began to talk. That was very interesting.

Where exactly were you while you were observing this?

I was close to Joao.

And how did you perceive the people during this process?

The people were all very unsettled and their power was like that of dwarves in comparison to my own perspective and my perception. That was very new to me and I was very curious. The energy fields of humans have many layers and I perceived the outermost layer. That was new to me. I had never experienced anything like it. Valdivino began his session and after a certain time, he left Joao's body and returned to our level. I then talked extensively to Oswaldo Cruz.

What exactly did he tell you?

He told me that the people needed our help and that here I had the possibility to help them.

What did you do then?

Then I continued to observe how the operations were performed on

144

the people. These operations are really very moving. I had never seen the like but I loved it and I realised that this would be a wonderful possibility to stay on my level and to be able to help at the same time.

So you did not wish to incarnate again?

No.

Why not?

The people were too wicked for my liking.

This wickedness, were you never able to forget that, not even in the other state of being?

No.

How is it now that you are helping the people?

Then I do not care whether they are wicked or nice, I help because I like to help and because this is my destiny.

Do you also enter Joao's body now?

Yes.

And how do you perceive the people through his eyes?

I still only perceive the outer layer but I can bring my own qual-

ity into play.

When you operate, how do you perceive that?

The operations are mostly performed by the other entities; I cannot really do this. Maybe one day I will, but I can not now. The entities that do that have progressed further in their understanding.

So you do not really perform operations?

No; most of the visible operations are performed by Augusto, Cruz and Valdivino.

What message would you like to give the people?

146

That they should please begin to open their hearts, it is like humanity has taken on the wrong shape. The people have a heart but they do not use it anywhere, this is crazy. This is like being an alien on this planet, one who does not really belong here, but you do belong here. This world is the right one for you; you have all the possibilities of the cosmos at your disposal in order to open your hearts and go into the energy of connection at last. These lives without connection make me very sad. That is not the meaning of life.
I am here in the love that I have always been searching for, but you, too, can live this love, it is so easy.
It is such a pity that I was so powerless in this respect, but finally I begin to see the reason behind all these functions, this is the process I am presently going through.

How do you feel?

Feelings as you know them do not exist here, but I am very much at ease. The love is everywhere over here, and respect. I need that.

I read that you take a lot of time to talk to the people, is this true?

Yes, the people always ask so many questions and I cannot refuse them answers, that is the way I am.

Then I say thank you very much now and I wish you well on your journey.

Thank you very much.

147

Chico Xavier

Francisco Cândido Xavier ("Chico" Xavier), born on April 2, 1910 in Pedro Leopolo, Minas Gerais and died on June 30, 2002 in Uberaba, Minas Gerais, was a revered Brazilian medium.

Joao de Deus received the information that his mission was to establish a healing facility in Abadiânia from the entity Bezerra de Menezes, channelled by Chico Xavier. During his lifetime and beyond, Chico Xavier has been a mentor to Joao de Deus. You can see a clear image of Chico Xavier, already deceased at the time, standing behind Joao de Deus in a photograph.

Chico Xavier had been in contact to spiritual entities from a very young age. During his lifetime, he published more than 400 books channelled by spiritual entities (psychography). He donated the proceeds of sales from these books to charitable organizations, which made him enormously popular. Xavier made spiritualism popular in Brazil through numerous appearances on radio and television. The number of believers in spiritualism (according to the definition coined by Allan Kardec) in Brazil is estimated to be 4.6 million people.

Chico Xavier gained international fame in 1979 when a message he channelled was accepted as evidence in a court case against a young man who was accused of having murdered his friend. The defendant was acquitted due to this message said to have come from his deceased friend.

∞

The documentary film "Chico Xavier – the movie" was screened in Brazil on Chico Xavier's 100th birthday on April 2, 2010. Directed by Daniel Folho, it is based on the biography "As Vidas de Chico Xavier" by the journalist Marcel Souto Maior. The number of viewers had reached the two million mark by week three.

Interview

I now ask the entity known to the people as Chico Xavier for an interview.

Yes, I am here; the energy is pleasant.

First of all, I would like to know how you are wherever you are at the moment.

I am well, not especially excited, but I am happy that you contacted me. I am very familiar with this form of writing.

Did you also work like that?

Yes.

Then maybe you can describe to me exactly what happens during this process.

You can empathize with the contacted entity to such a degree that its thoughts are yours. This is like feeding energy into a shell. Then this shell begins to write.

This means that in a way, you are inside me now?

That is not quite correct.
The energy that is me is not completely inside you but I am connected to you and your being can read my thoughts. This is similar

but not quite the same, you understand?

Yes, I understand that, I am so strongly connected to you that I can read your energy very clearly.

Yes, exactly.

Did you work in the same way?

Yes.

What exactly is the talent in this?

Only those can do this whose energy is very pure because the channel has to be clear. You might say that we come from a long way away and we need really clear channels in order to make the long distance that we have to travel practically nonexistent in this communication.

151

I am curious as to how this distance is finally bridged?

This is like with a lemon that you peel and then you reach the spiritual form. There are many networks and pathways in this form and the centre is the core. But when the channel is clear, it is as if you pierce through the rind and the peel with a needle to reach the core directly.

I heard that you had very bad eyes. I also have problems with such symptoms, is there a connection? To the gift and the physical symptoms?

∞

No, the eyesight is not linked to this type of connection; that is different. The eyesight is a physical thing. Either the body can deal with the energy or it can't and with me, it couldn't. It was hard for me but I accepted it.

Then please tell me about your last lifetime.
Were you predominantly in contact with the deceased?

No, similarly as with you, I did not deal only with this part, but with the part of the other worlds as well. I also could enter into many layers.

Did you have to deal with the problem of having to protect yourself, the way I have?

A little differently; I was at home in a different energy and therefore I had fewer dealings with the deceased. But I, also, was always called upon to protect myself.

Did you take money for your work at that time?

No, working on this mission is nothing that can be paid for with money, that would not be right. Of course some people gave me money but I was never in the expectation that I was to receive money for this. It is not right, if you are connected.

With whom did you communicate most?

I communicated most with the Wise Brotherhood; that is also your source, right?

Yes.

Would you like to tell me about your transition?

I was in a state of peace and I knew that it would be over soon. The friends had told me. That did not worry me, but I was excited nevertheless. The beginning direct perception was much clearer.

What exactly did you perceive?

The entities became very clearly perceptible to me, much more than ever before. This is as if another layer had been removed. Then in my dream I went to another level and everyone was there.

You mean to say you fell asleep and you died?

Yes...

Were you afraid?

Hardly at all, it was the uncertainty of perception, because I had lived in increasing darkness all my life and I was a little apprehensive of what it would be like when I could suddenly see clearly again.

And what was it like?

The feeling was very nice. I felt the love within that light and this energy was so healing, so connecting and such pure joy.

Author's note:
The feeling is like being reborn, I am filled with a deep euphoria, as if I was a child again and excited to be allowed to play and be happy after a long abstinence.

I feel your energy and I have to cry, why is that?

> *That is the joy and a little bit the sadness that I had never been able to feel like this during my entire life.*

Author's note:
I have to cry very hard, there are floods of tears and I am deeply, deeply sad. Although few words are needed to describe this, the feelings involved are very intense. He is really crying bitterly.

154   I do understand you, but this is now over for you, isn't it?

> *I am a little wistful in that respect...*

I understand – what saddens you most?

> *The perception that you are given through the healthy eyes is a way of experiencing beauty and I did not have that beauty ...*

And, where you are now, what does it look like there?

> *The energy is very high and wise; I am using its power to move.*

And how do you move – with your thoughts?

∞

No, that is not quite correct, it is the potentials that we create in ourselves that move us. In other words, I formulate the intent and then I determine the movement.

How can I visualize this, do you fly or do you walk?

You cannot compare this with human movement. I just move.

Do you have a body? What does it look like?

Oval in certain respects.

And what is its colour?

White.

155

I have heard that during your lifetime you were Joao's mentor and it was you who told him to come here.

Yes, that was the entity Bezerra.

Did Joao come to you?

Yes, he wanted to know how he should work and where.

And Bezerra then told you where.

Yes.

And do you know now, from your current perspective, why here in

Abadiânia?

Because the energy of the place is very special.

And do you know why this is so?

No.

Did you never ask yourself why?

Be connected and you will know it.

I once heard that there are or were many crystals below the surface of the earth…?

Yes.

And have been for a long time?

Time as you know it does not exist here; time is a disc; I can turn it. The place remains in its energy because it pulsates in the energy, and this is much older than the crystals that have come into being because of the energy. This is not a thing that disappears; it is IN-SIDE the earth…

Somebody else has told me that Brazil is governed by a female chakra.

Yes.

Does this chakra rule here as well?

No.

Then what does?

The earth's energy is very open and pure here, it is like a hole in the energy surrounding the earth, and that allows entities from the other levels to come here, and that amplifies the energy, it is a synergy that supports itself in perpetuity.

How did you find Joao after your passing?

I simply went to him, that is very easy, you just think of someone and you receive the impulse to find him, this really was a matter of hardly any time at all if you want to measure it like that.

How did you perceive Abadiânia then?

I saw it bathed in white light; this is a very rare thing. Mostly, the surface of the earth is very dark.

How did you go inside Joao for the first time?

That was very easy, he sensed my presence and then called my name, and then I went inside him.

How did you perceive his aura?

The aura was big and wide; he was like a balloon.

And how do you perceive the people that come before you?

∞

The people protect their problems more than themselves – I perceive their desperation and their fear. It took a while for me to study this form of perception but I picked it up quickly enough.

And what exactly do you perceive? How do you see these fears?

The fears are black or brown, the desperation is green, the self pity is like a layer above all these colours; it is difficult to describe because there are not really words to describe this.

Are there things that make you sad looking at the people here?

The people still don't do much of the work, they still think that we are doing everything, but that is not the case, we enter Joao in order to tell them what to do and then they still don't do it right. It is the way of doing it, not the doing as such. The perception of the people is too closed off for my liking; this is not good, I would like to tear everyone's heart open so that they understand where their troubles come from...

Oh, you have said this well.

No, that is not well, Sylvia, that is very sad, but I am trying my best to understand it...

But are there any beautiful moments in all this?

Yes, the people who open their hearts and finally experience healing, they are the gift; this is why I do this.

Would you like to come back to earth?

Yes.

Why?

I want to see clearly, want to enjoy more with my eyes.

But do you have an answer as to why you had this affliction during your lifetime?

That is a good question; the clear view that I did not have was the key to the opening of my soul into the energies that made me write; unfortunately, that is the truth. I have paid this price in order to fulfil this mission.

159

And now you want to live a life during which you can celebrate life seeing clearly and strongly through your own eyes?

Yes.

But there is much suffering on earth, there is the risk that when you come back to earth that you will be afflicted by another harm?

That may be, but I would choose to avoid that. In my last life, I chose the eye topic in order not to stray from the path of connection. I wanted to walk this path and it did not happen by accident.

Dear Chico, do you perceive all the other entities?

Yes, of course.

Do you communicate with each other?

Yes.

Do you have friends?

I am friendly with all of them; most of them have been in this form for a long time but I admire their devotion as if it were the first day for them.

When the operations are performed, what do you perceive?

Just as you have already experienced it, I recognize the energies, how they are being accelerated through energy; that is all.

160

Would you like to leave a message for the people?

Yes, I would like that very much.
The people who come here, they should walk in peace and mind-fulness please and listen to the silence.
Healing here is not to be found in communication with other people but through opening up to the messages that we give them constantly. The people are too distracted, even here and especially here. This is a place of silence. Perpetual silence.

Yes, I can understand that.

The perception of the place and the energies here will grow ex-

ponentially when communication amongst the people ceases and they silently listen...

Do you also perceive the shining orbs?

Yes, they are funny, they move so fast and move the energies fast as well, that is all so colourful, I love to watch them, most of them are all white but there are also other colours among them, that is wonderful to watch.
The white orbs take the energy away from the soul and shine it. Then they give these parts back into the soul.

And you, the other entities, how do you work?

We take the energy from the people, that which is negative, into our energy fields and cleanse it; then we give that energy back.

161

And that happens very fast?

Yes.

When one of you is in Joao, where are the others?

We are on our level and work from there.

And that works the same way as right now, when the two of us communicate, you are on your level and we are connected to each other; you are in your level and then connect to those who need an operation... So you are not all of you in those rooms, but you direct your consciousness into this level, to these people here... so you really only

∞

come into these rooms when you incorporate?

Yes.

So why can Joao not work like the two of us now, just by transmitting messages like you are just now transmitting to me?

That would not be enough, because then his perception would not be enough. He is clairvoyant but he cannot read energy fields, but we can do that through him.

Have you got any idea what will happen when he is no longer around?

I do not know that yet, but I have a hunch; we will be able to incorporate into very pure persons and continue to work as before.

162

But that will be at different places.

I do not know that exactly yet.
Most people will need a little more time for that.

Do you have a favourite place in the *Casa*?

No.

Are you in contact to Dom Ignacio?

Yes, but he is relatively isolated, he needs this type of concentration.

Can you perceive entities other than those that have been communicated to me up to now?

No.

Did you ever perform an operation on a human body?

No, I do not dare to do that; it is too physical for my liking.

Can you confirm that here, the white orbs reach up to the sky in the shape of a pyramid?

Yes.

Are there any other helping energy bodies here?

163

No, the orbs are multifaceted enough.

What happens when a so-called miracle healing takes place?

This type of healing is no miracle. We take the energies and transform them and sometimes the body begins to react immediately.

Why is this not the case with most people?

I do not know, perhaps Solomon will be able to tell you more about this.

Joao once said that healing was a reward, do you see this the same way?

No, I see it differently. Healing for me is not a reward but you have to want this healing.

Whom else should I talk to under all circumstances?

"The silent form" – it is a part of Abadiânia ... it is the force that protects Abadiânia.

I thank you with all my heart for this wonderful interview.

Thank you, my dear.

Oswaldo Cruz

Oswaldo Cruz was born in 1872 in Sao Luiz do Paraitinga, Sao Paolo. He was extraordinarily intelligent and was able to read and write at the young age of five. His family moved to Rio de Janeiro in 1877 where at the age of 15, he went to study medicine. As a student he published two works on microbiology. In 1892, at the age of 20, he graduated summa cum laude with his thesis on "The Movements of Microbes through Water." In 1893, he married Emilia Fonseca, who came from a wealthy family of local merchants. They had three children.

He travelled to France in 1896, where he worked for three years at the Pasteur Institute. He was highly respected by his colleagues for his intelligence and for his dedication to microbiology. In spite of the Institute's invitation to stay, he went back to his native Brazil in 1899, which in those days was considered "a huge infirmary". He accepted the invitation to head the Hygienic Institute to help fight the bubonic plague that was ravaging the seaport of Santos at the time.

When the Federal Serotherapy Institute was established in the vicinity of Rio de Janeiro, the Brazilian Government asked the Pasteur Institute to send one of their members in order to lead the efforts to develop new vaccines to fight the disease. The Institute informed them that one of their most qualified members, Oswaldo Cruz, was already living in Brazil.

In 1900, he was invited to conduct a health assessment in the states of Amazonas (the railway line Madeira – Mamore) and Para (Belem). He directed the **sanitation campaign in the state of Amazonas.**

Oswaldo Cruz received numerous national and international honours and was elected into the Brazilian Academy of Letters.

In 1916, he left his post in Petropolis as a sick and tired man and was elected prefect of the town. However, he stepped back from this position before his term ran out because his tireless political campaigning for the common good was conflicting with his private life.

He died in 1917 at the age of 44, leaving a foundation which produced sixty percent of the world's vaccines.

(Source: Spiritual Healing, Ismar E. Garcia)

Interview

I call the energy that was known to mankind as Oswaldo Cruz. Dear Oswaldo. You are surely aware that I would like to interview all of you in order to find out who you once were and who you are now. I have read a lot about you and I learned that you were very intelligent and went to university at a young age. Please tell me how you perceived the world.

> *As a young boy, I never understood the people and their way to see the world. It was alien to me because to me they were as if in a state of sleep, always only half conscious.*

And were you able to perceive spiritual things at that time?

> *No, but I could see the energy of the people in so far as that I could see they were as if encrusted.*

Do you have any idea where your extraordinary intelligence came from?

> *That was inside me, the special kind of connection that I had was very energetic, that is true. This energy was the reason why I understood so much at such a young age.*

How would you describe this special kind of connection?

> *The energy that coursed through me was not just energy, it was cosmic energy, which does not flow in this way very often.*

∞

What exactly is this power, what are the conditions that make it flow like that?

> *The power of the mind is the decisive factor. The energy needs a channel and the mind has to create it. I brought this channel with me and that was the reason for such things.*

But cosmic energy everywhere originates from the source. Do you mean you had a special gift to channel this power?

> *Yes.*

Could you translate it in this way, that this high energy was able to transform the cells and ultimately, allowed the brain to function more actively?

> *Yes, but I would also maintain that there are other components to this. The forming of the cells is not the only thing that happens, it is the special characteristic of this power to make it possible to see things differently. Consciousness is the decisive factor – it allows you to perceive differently in this energy.*

Having such a consciousness, how did you deal with people who were very encrusted and were living without awareness?

> *That was very difficult; to me the people were as if they came from another planet. I wanted to tell them something and they never understood.*

Did that make you sad?

No, but I didn't know why that was so and why they were like this. Sometimes this was a little problematic.

But in the final analysis they recognised parts of you and they even gave you honours for it?

Yes, but I was not on earth in order to receive honours. I wanted to bring something to humanity. This knowledge was my mission, not the awards.

I have heard that you were also interested in microbiology and that you were very successful. Why were you fascinated by microbiology of all things?

Good question, but to me these forms of existence were very interesting. I wanted to show to the people that there is a connection between microbiology and consciousness; this is as if you would take the small beings to talk about the big beings. Microelements are all very simple and very easily influenced; this facilitates the clarification of the general principles.

169

Are there any special moments in your life that defined you?

The decision of the people that I should return to Brazil was my deliverance. I had never really wanted to travel far, but I had to go away sometimes in order to spread this knowledge, but when I was able to work in Brazil, I was very calm and settled in my energy. I enjoyed this way of working because it was more protected.

And how did you feel then?

I was very happy and in my element. I wanted more and more to help the people in this way.

Did you have wife and child?

Yes.

What were your encounters with women like? Often these are very intuitive and therefore more connected, but that does not necessarily mean that they are more aware than other people.

That was very difficult, because often they were living in a very unaware fashion. I found this fact very suspect. On the one hand they were very charming, on the other hand very unaware and through this sometimes very loveless; it was like in a clown circus – one of their masks was love and the other was wickedness, and both were part of one and the same person.

But finally, you found someone?

Yes, my wife was very lovely.

Were you able to pass on the gift of your special energy to your children?

No, this soul quality was my own; I don't know whether you can pass on the like and what would be necessary to do this.

May I ask you about your passing?

170

No, I would like to keep that to myself.

Please tell me from the point on that you would like to talk about. I would just like to find a connection, from the human form into the new form as an entity – and why everything has come to be as it is now?

I had arrived on the level of the Ascended Masters and there, I asked myself what I could do that would make sense. The people still needed help and I wanted to continue to help. But I no longer wanted to be in a human body. Then I met Valdivino and he began to show me how the entities worked with Joao. He showed me Joao's form in a session and I understood how it worked. Then I also incorporated in him and started to work from there.

And what was that like?

That was very exhausting. The shape of Joao is very small compared to my own power and I had to constrict myself a little in my energy.

What was it like to look through his eyes then? How did you perceive the people?

That was very interesting. The images I saw there were not comparable to that which I had known before. Energy fields were visible inside the people that I could now see especially clearly, and through this I was able to treat the causes of the illnesses. That was a wonderful experience.

Can you send me an image of how you perceive them?

The energies are in the people and in the aura; you cannot sepa-rate this. It is difficult to describe. Words are not really enough to describe this. You have to imagine this like a matrix, which is con-vertible in its energy; that needs time but it is possible and we here give the impulses in order to transform this energy.

How exactly does the cause of an illness look to you? How do recog-nise illness?

That is the dark energy. I see much more than just dark energy. It is like a special type of energy that is not healthy. This is difficult to describe, you know it when you see it. This energy is not healthy and then you want to make this energy healthy.

When do you decide that a person needs to go into the current or that he needs an operation?

It is the energy of the person. When they are strong enough they re-ceive an operation. If they are still weak in their energy, they have to meditate first. This is like a preparation for the operation.

There are many people who say that the current is also healing. How would you describe the current, what exactly happens there according to your perception?

It is like a light connection that the people receive. The energy flows through the room and through this through the people, and that makes them slowly convalesce in their energy. Then, when they are ready for an operation, we operate. That is, as already mentioned, always different.

∞

And how do you perceive the operations?

Exactly like the others.

Do you like performing visible operations?

Yes.

Where did you get this knowledge?

From our perspective here working on your body is not really comparable to a normal operation in your hospitals. It is completely different and I have watched Dr Augusto and I understand what exactly he is doing.

And how would you describe this in your own words?

173

The energy he feeds into the bodies is pure soul energy. You do not have to have a complete understanding of internal medicine in order to do this and to understand this. The only hurdle is the cut into the body and that is a matter of practice. The first time was a little difficult for me, but I managed with the help of Dr Augusto. Then it was fine. The difficult thing is that the body of the human being is very small. And it feels to me as if I were cutting into the tissue of a mouse.

But when you are incorporated in Joao, aren't the proportions corresponding to human perception?

That is true, but my perception of energy is different.

∞

And is it also like this when you do the eye operations?

It is similar; we have to be incredibly delicate in order to do this.

Is there something that bothers you when you work visually in the *Casa*?

No, that is impossible. I am so highly focused then that I can tune out everything else. Joao's physicality is a little peculiar, but I am happy to be able to do it like this.

Can you tell me how you feel when you do this work?

That is difficult to describe, but I will try. The people need to know that we do not judge them when we cleanse them. The perception of our world does not deal in judgement. You can imagine this as if you were looking at a collection of eggs before you: they all look the same but some are of a different colour... some eggs are larger, but in the final analysis they are all eggs.

So you do not even perceive a person's personality?

Exactly.

And you're not even interested in it?

Exactly.

So you have no emotions doing this?

Yes, but still we perceive... in a multileveled way.

And yet, are there things that make you sad doing this work?

Yes, when I have to observe how the people do not really partici-pate. The way you concentrate on something is the decisive factor in how it accelerates, but there are people here whose thoughts are not really on the work at hand.

What do you think is the reason for this?

The reason is connected to many things. It is the fact that the peo-ple here are not alone, but are steeped in all sorts of distractions through communication amongst each other, and it is the fact that the people are supposed to be especially protected here, but we do not protect them from their destiny. The path that they walk is their own path, we can only give impulses but when they do not imple-ment them it is out of our hands. I would like to emphasize this once more: The responsibility and the exceptional environment demand their highest concentration here.

175

Is there a type of work you especially like doing here?

Yes, the operations in the energy room, the invisible operations, I like doing them very much. It is beautiful to watch how the energy grows there. You have to imagine, the people come in to have this operation and are relatively small in their power... then we come with our consciousness and heal the energy... and in the process, their aura gets bigger and they become wider; it is as if you were

∞

watering the flowers. The power grows wider and larger – always wonderful to watch.

There are people who have to have many operations. Why is this so; why isn't one enough?

This is a good question. I have the following answer to this: People always need a little time in order to realise what happens. The energies also need a little time in order to work in all layers and spheres of activity. All of this in turn needs time in order to manifest into matter and during this time the people begin to create new blockages with their beliefs and thoughts; this is the reason why we then have to operate again.

Is it possible for people to reverse the entire healing process after an operation just through their old belief patterns?

Yes.

What can we tell them in order to prevent this from happening?

That they should not go into their old patterns please; whenever they realise that things are returning to what they used to be, they should change that; it is really quite simple.

What is the reason, why do they make it so complicated?

It is impossible to describe, I never understood this during my life and I do not understand it now – it just is what it is. They are like that and they will probably stay this way for a long time to come.

∞

Do you have a particular attitude toward the church?

The church is a thorn in my side because on the one hand, it is a good idea, but they go about it the wrong way. I would like to say something about that:
The energy that flows through people is a free energy. The soul needs this freedom and it needs the openness. The people are able to live this openness but institutions like the Catholic Church for example are not concerned with supporting people in their openness; this is a pity, because in principle, they do not teach bad things.

But aren't there people even inside the Church who are connected and knowledgeable about energy?

Yes; it is surely a question of power. If you liberate the people, you no longer have any power over them; maybe this is the reason for the church's problems, because if it wants power, it is not connected. The church would have many thousands more followers if it only was truthful and free, but the current type of teaching is not good.

Are you sure that you want me to pass on these messages? Many people need their religious beliefs and they cling to them in order to survive.

Yes, that's right, but you're not here in order to tell people about the things they want to hear. Your task is to communicate knowledge in its basic truth and not in the form that people would like to hear it.

What do you like about Dom Ignacio?

His way of doing things is very powerful and I like this; I like entities that do not think in limitations. He had been like this already as a human being and is even more so now as a spiritual entity. He knows no bounds and he lives this, and that is incredible to behold. It shows in the way he approaches and helps the people. I notice time and again how he observes them long after their operations are done and how he is there for them; this is incredibly considerate.

If you could measure him in terms of strength, where would you place Dom Ignacio?

He would be one of the most powerful; and after that Dr Augusto; then Pereido and then myself.

How do you perceive the white orbs?

They are very beautiful to behold. They are the little helpers at our side; we need them.

What exactly are they doing according to your perception?

That is easy to describe, they cleanse the energy fields when only light cleansing is needed. That is charming to behold. They take the energy, cleanse it and then give it back.

How do they cleanse it without arms and hands?

The "devour" it and then the energy re-emerges in a neutral state, this is quite incredible to behold.

∞

What do you think… have these orbs been here all the time?

I believe they are an integral part of the earth. I believe they are a composite form, bound to the energy of the earth on one hand and dependent on taking nourishment from the sun, but ethereal on the other hand. It is not easy for me to explain that.

Is there a place in the *Casa* that you especially like?

No, I like being on my level and I like working in all spaces in the Casa from here, that is all and that is fine like that… but I do not have a favourite place there.

Do you often direct your consciousness into the *Casa*?

Yes, and often to Joao.

What do you prefer, to incorporate into Joao or to operate from your own level?

That is a good question; I'll have to think about that. The operations are beautiful to watch, but is it also wonderful to look at the auric fields… see the many different shapes… you cannot compare this, so I cannot answer the question.

Would you like to give the people who come here to walk the path of healing another message?

That they please, please, please, please go into this process more consciously. This is not a vacation.

∞

What makes you especially happy?

To observe when people are truly healing. This is like a rebirth, their energy begins to flow and it is like a fountain; where there was no energy before, energy now flows and begins to live, it is incredibly beautiful.

Do you miss some aspect of being human?

It is difficult for me to say, it is so beautiful in this state of existence that I do not miss much about being human, but let us say the physical pleasures, the sensual side is missing, but only a little.

What sensual pleasure do you miss most? Kissing? Eating? Or what?

Kissing is not as important as people think, but eating, that is very nice.

Would you like to be incarnate again?

No, this form is wonderful and I can help the people much better from here than I was able to as a human being. In those days, it was even more difficult to gain attention for this type of knowledge, but from here, I can do as and how I like without being looked at curiously, as it happened to me when I was alive; I no longer have to deal with judgment concerning my work.

Do you know why you died so young?

I believe this was a question of energy, my lifestyle did not really support this energy and so it began to retreat; this retreat resulted in my death. I should have supported this energy more.

Well, with this, I have come to the end of my questions and would like to thank you very much for your great answers and for your trust.

Thank you.

King Solomon

King Solomon was the second son of King David. According to the Bible, he reigned over Israel for 40 years (970–930 BC). Solomon was known for his administrative genius, he built roads and encouraged trade; his trade routes extended far beyond the boundaries of his kingdom.

Although he commanded a large army, he preferred negotiations to warfare; he was adept in keeping the peace and preventing war.

Through meditation, Solomon acquired cosmic awareness, which allowed him to distinguish between negative and positive energy. His free will allowed him to use a positive attitude, to leave the negative behind and to concentrate instead on the positive side of knowledge.

Although there are many legends about this subject, it seems to be true that "King Solomon's Mines" allowed him to support a lifestyle in splendour. Extensive archaeological studies found the ruins of a fortified city in the middle of the African jungle. Abandoned mines in its vicinity support the belief that this was indeed the fabled city of Ophir, said to be the source of King Solomon's fabulous gold.

King Solomon is a constant presence in the history of the freemasons. His temple is one of the symbolic foundations of their beliefs and rituals.

Historically, Solomon is known for his acute sense of justice. In his judgments, he always sought to give to each his own.
One of his most famous judgments was passed in the dispute of two

women over a child whom each woman claimed as her own. In order to end the dispute, Solomon ordered to have the child cut in half and to give each woman her share. The real mother immediately begged that the child be given to the other woman. King Solomon then declared that the child be handed over to that woman, because only a mother would put her child's life above her own interest.

There are two biblical books ascribed to King Solomon.

(Source: Spiritual Healing, Ismar E. Garcia)

Interview

Dear King Solomon, I sense a lot of love with you and it moves me to tears, why is that?

I am so happy that you are contacting me.

So these are tears of joy?

Yes, these are tears of joy.

Why?

The people never understand me and I am so full of joy to be given the possibility to send them messages.

Author's note:
It is as if my heart were a thousand times bigger and as if there were no division between the body and the cosmos and that "I am" only this energy that we feel in our hearts. It is an interesting sensation because it is not sadness, yet what I feel is very intense…

Dear King Solomon, please tell me where I can reach you?

You will find me on the fifth level.

I learnt from the Wise Brotherhood that the fifth level is the level of the Guardian energies, is this right?

Yes that is right, the guardians are also here, but I am here as well and many others. We are there in order to protect the energy.

How do you do this?

That is not easy to explain, the energy of the cosmos has free will. This can also create negativity sometimes. In order for this not to happen to excess, a kind of guardian energy is needed and this is here and operates from here.

So you become active whenever a lot of negativity is being created in the cosmos?

Yes, exactly.

So you are also active when people are destroying each other in a further act of unawareness – with wars or acts of terror and the like?

Yes, we seek to cleanse the all-directing energy that makes this possible after this has happened and thus we do not create too much negative energy.

So you are dampening the resonances somewhat?

Yes, exactly.

Dear King Solomon, I am really happy that I can speak to you now. Is the way I am doing this good for you?

Yes it is. You are always connected to me and this is your gift; this

∞

is why we will be able to talk much to one another.

May I ask you now about your last lifetime? I have read about you that you were very wise in your judgments. Have you always been like that or did you have special teachers that conveyed this wisdom to you?

I was always like that, I came to earth and was always very connected with the astral worlds as you call them.

How did you perceive the people when you were a human being?

The people were very unaware and I experienced this as very painful, because their words were as arrows for me.

But you were a king, therefore it must have been much easier for you than for someone who was lower in the human hierarchy and therefore would have been treated with even less respect?

Yes, that may be, but even on my level the people were not very respectful and loving to each other. Unfortunately this is not bound to social levels but is all pervading.

Were your parents unloving towards you?

No, they were loving.

Was there something that touched you especially during your lifetime?

My mother's love and kindness; she was very wise and taught me many important lessons during my time as a king. This was really important because otherwise I would have been lost due to my sensitivity.

Did you have a special feeling for the spiritual world?

No, my intuition was my perception.

So you were always led by your feelings?

Yes.

Were you always able to utilise this or was that not always possible?

Life is a constant up and down of conflict and flow; that is how it is. Sometimes there were more conflicts, sometimes less.

There is an old story about you in which you judged very wisely in a dispute between the two women.

Yes I know, the people like this story.

Was there anything else that you especially like to remember?

Yes, there was a lot, in principle I was very happy and I was able to live my energy fully; that was very beautiful.

Did you have wife and children?

Yes, that was wonderful, I would have liked to have more children, but it was not possible because of her.

And what made you saddest during your lifetime?

The cruelty of the people towards each other.

Then let us move on with your story. Would you like to tell me about your passing?

Yes.

What happened after you left your body?

188

The energy that was I turned into another form in the process of leaving the body. This happened like this: I used to experience the people as bodies but also as energy because of the feelings through which I perceived. After I left the body I was in the world of feeling and devotion. Through this I was suddenly able to perceive the energies much more clearly. The energies were different, sometimes colourful, sometimes cold, sometimes warm, sometimes peaceful.

You felt colours?

That is a funny question; yes, I saw and felt it that way.

How did you perceive the human bodies in this state, outside of your body?

It was just energy that I perceived now, not the shapes of their human bodies.

In which "environment" did you receive the energy of the people?

Around them it was even darker than the energy itself; it was like a sea of mud in which the energy dwelled. This mud was always equally thick.

Were you afraid?

No, the energy inside you knows no fear; it is the ego that is afraid.

What happened then?

Then I felt drawn to another perception. I wanted to feel the purity again that I had felt before, that is why I moved away from this state and started on the path to the fifth level.

What did this path look like, did this happen quickly, did it happen slowly?

189

It happened relatively slowly. I wanted to visit the individual levels and understand them.

Please tell me about that.

It is as if you are flying upwards in steps. I stopped again and again and looked closely at what I saw. The first level was the dark layer of mud. The next level was already lighter and I already felt better. There were many types of energy here similar to those that I perceived amongst the humans, but they were not surrounded by so much negativity. The environment was much lighter and more positive.

Did you want to communicate with them?

No, just to observe. I knew where I was.

According to your knowledge, where were you?

In the world of the deceased who vibrate lighter and higher.

And then?

Then I went into the second level, those of the angels. This is where the many small orbs of light come from.

Oh really?

190

Yes, the orbs were very lovely to look at, that was very beautiful, I liked watching them, this freedom, this peacefulness and joy that they emanate is wonderful. This is probably the reason why people have given that name to these orbs: the angels.

And what were the orbs doing?

The orbs were moving and dancing to and fro. Sometimes a Master came and took them with him.

Oh, was this like: "Please come with me and help me with my mission?"

Yes, exactly.

How did you perceive these Masters, what did they look like?

They are oval shaped energies, in the terms of your geometry, that visit those orbs. Those orbs then flocked around the oval energies and followed them. Then they went into another area, I could not see this any more.

And then?

Then I ascended further, a little higher, and looked around there.

And what did you perceive there?

There I perceived the Ascended Masters. There were many, many master energies. It is like a sea of oval energies that appears vast and powerful. It is very imposing.

191

Did you ever check what your own body looks like in this perception?

That is a good question; no, it was not yet in my perception that I could also have a body myself. My interests were elsewhere at the time.

Were you able to communicate with the Masters?

Hmm... The perception of the masters was very intensely engaged with human beings and with other beings in the cosmos.

One moment, you mean to say with this that the masters are active on all planets and not just looking after the humans, right?

Yes, exactly.

How can a master act, and what exactly does he do then, did you manage to find that out on your journey?

The masters can only do something when they are called. That happens via prayer and direct invocations.

And how do the masters work?

When they are called, they first direct their attention towards this wish or prayer, and it is only then that they react. It depends on the nature of the invoking energy: if it is pure they can act faster, if it is contaminated, helpers are needed.

Ah, and is it then that the shining orbs are doing their work?

Yes, exactly.

That means when a master wants to implement something, then he calls the orbs to his side in order to cleanse the energy that is calling?

Yes, exactly. He directs the orbs into the parts of this person that have to be cleansed. It is only then that he can act. The degree of contamination determines the effect that the cosmic power can achieve.

And when they have fulfilled the wish or the desire, does the Masters' perception then return to their own energy?

Yes.

Once more please in order to clarify this for the people who prefer to think in terms of space. The energies of the Masters remain in their own state, on their level, but they move their consciousness, their intention, right?

Yes, that is right. The Masters need a certain kind of energy in order to be able to incorporate into bodies, that is rarely the case; this is why they remain on their level; but they direct their concentration and attention onto your plane.

And what is this like in the case of the shining orbs? They really do come to earth, don't they?

Yes exactly, they are all able to come to earth at all times, but they cannot always start to work immediately. That is another thing altogether. The people are surrounded by this layer of mud and the angels, as you call them, need a little more time in order get into this layer. This is why it is easier to work in a place like this one (Abadiânia) than in other places, because there is not this layer of mud.

And what happened then?

I wanted to look further, and that is what I did. That is why I went on to the next level. The fourth. On this level, there are also Masters but those are different entities. This is where the higher energies of these masters work in special functions, with special qualities.

193

∞

What did you perceive there?

This is where I perceived the energy of Dom Ignacio; the way he works with his energy in the world of humans. That was very interesting and I observed this very carefully. The people were close to him, but he was on this level, he was like a string that reached onto their plane. It is difficult to describe with words.

Author's note: He sends me an image showing Dom Ignacio directing his attention to the human beings and how the humans look up at him. He is vibrating very highly and appears to be above them but very connected to them. The humans seek him and he is seeking them, but all of this appears to happen on and most of all through different levels; hence the image of the thread. It is indeed really difficult to describe. Even I find it very hard now to describe the image that he sent me.

Dear King Solomon, but you passed over much earlier in the reckoning of human history than Dom Ignacio; so how do you explain this?

Yes, that is true, but Dom Ignacio was already in this energy at the time of my passing, even if he himself chose to incarnate a few more times. I perceived him in this power, independently of the incarnations and of how you perceive his work today.

And when you observed him, was he in a state of incarnation at the time?

Yes.

That means that you perceived his higher consciousness but his energy was inside an organism?

Yes.

And what happened then?

I observed him further but I also ascended onto a higher level. That is the level from which I am talking to you now. It is the region of the stabilised energies. I stayed there, there was no higher stage for me; this was the last level that I could perceive.

I seem to remember that Chico Xavier insisted that you are also a member of the Wise Brotherhood? But that is located on the sixth level, isn't it?

This is correct, but the Wise Brotherhood works through several levels. This begins on the fourth level and this is why Chico's perception is correct, but I am not with them the whole time but I work from this level into the subject matter that is being worked upon.

195

So how do you perceive the Wise Brotherhood?

I cannot perceive them fully, but I experience them as very white and very light.

How did you feel on the fifth level?

That was very beautiful, I was surrounded by energies that wanted to help; it is as if you are welcomed into a family who has the same intention.

∞

But don't all of the energies on the higher levels wish to help - the angels, the Masters, the Brotherhood and so forth?

That is correct, but for me this energy was the right one.

And now you work from this level and you do not wish to incarnate any more?

No, I don't need it, I can work from here; I prefer this; the wickedness of the humans is a very particular thing.

Would you like to describe to me what it looks like up there where you work?

That is easy: it is light and beautiful.

196

Do you perceive landscapes?

Yes, but the shapes are a little different; we also have a kind of landscape, but it is more like a kind of cloud landscape, all is soft and light.

Are there any colours?

No, not like that...

How many are you?

We are very many, but that is not relevant.

Then let us look at Abadiânia. How exactly did it happen that you came to incorporate into Joao?

Work on my level comes with high responsibility. I was looking for a change and I wanted to visit this being again that I had found so fascinating on the other, lower plane. That is why I went to this plane once more and I saw what this being was like over there. I spoke to him and he explained to me how he worked. He was the institution that created the pathways to connect the work on spiritual and material levels. Then I observed how he went into the body of Joao.

So you were not the first one to enter the body of Joao?

No, he showed me how it worked but I was the first one to be in Joao's body when he started to perceive this consciously.

You have to imagine this like a conversation about special communication. The energy that is Dom Ignacio builds bridges, that means that he found Joao, he recognized him amongst the humans as a wide-open soul and he began to prepare him to open even further. Then he was ready and I began the incorporations. That was the way.

So you collaborated on this path from the start.

Yes, that is right.
Dom Ignacio did not have to explain to me how this works, when I saw what Joao was like. He is soft and open. We use this quality in order to go into him.

And how does that feel?

That is an interesting question. Sensation is not given to us anymore in principle; not the way you know it in an organism, but it is a perception that still actually exists for us when we are inside him. It is relatively easy for us to occupy his energy, but when we are inside him we tend to feel very constricted. It is as if you were being stuffed into a pram. It is much too tight.

How is your perception different when you are inside him?

A good question; this is very important. When I am inside him, then I see the people and their energy bodies. That is the channel in which I read where the illness originated.

How do you see these images?

That is different. One person has many colours, the other not so many colours, but it is always a dark colour that signifies the reason for the illness.

Can you see a person's past?

No.

The future?

Yes... (hesitantly). The future is only the potential of the moment in which I see the people.

Do you perform operations?

Yes, but I prefer the invisible operations. The principle is always the same; the energy is cleansed and then put back into the body. In my case this is a different energy than in the case of the others, because I work from a different level, but it is always the same principle. The quality of the entity is always the right one for the person who receives it.

How do you perceive the operations?

The operations are like a cloud that is beginning to grow out of the person; like a fire that they have lit. It is a great joy for me to observe this.

Is there a place in the Casa that you like especially?

199

The chapel.

Can we meet you there?

At any rate it is easier to call me from there; the energy there is very pleasant for me.

There is a prayer triangle on the back wall of the operation room that is dedicated to you. Isn't it better for the people to call you from there?

This triangle is fine but the triangle in the chapel is much more powerful. Therefore please communicate to the people that they should leave their prayers there.

What else would you like to tell me?

The people have to learn that love is the key for the bliss that they seek through all their efforts outside of themselves. This is really important. To this very day I do not understand why people live their lives in such a way that allows some of them to die without love.

What else would you like to tell people?

That we are always there for the people, but that we need the power of their devotion and their love in order to really be able to work. If a person is closed off, it is impossible even for us to work on them. But even this is part of the process of experience that the soul wants to go through and has decided upon completely on its own and by the power of free will. Only you can decide to undergo the transformation, we cannot.

200

How do you perceive the place of Abadiânia?

It is the cleanest energy in the cosmos I have ever known to be on a planet.

Have you ever worked on other planets? And if so, how? Are they all as unaware as the human beings?

The other beings are further along in their development and do not need as much help as human beings, but they still need assistance.

Can you see whether some of them are still on earth or come to visit again and again?

Yes, some, but they are intelligent and hide their presence from you; this is important in order not to disturb you. The past has brought much misfortune to mankind, when other intelligences came here. So cosmic laws were established so that disturbances of this kind cannot not happen anymore.

What sort of disturbances occurred?

Humankind was still very unaware but not as yet contaminated. That only happened through impulses from the more intelligent beings that were not given in harmony with your consciousness, this is why the world that you know was created by the intelligences and your truth. It is not easy to explain, but in any case you have been manipulated.

201

But how could this happen, that whole planets and their people can be manipulated and not allowed to grow out of and by themselves according to the cosmic laws?

Unfortunately, I do not know that. I was not present at this event, but I know that it created much misery in the cosmos.

What is your perception of the religions on mother earth in their current energy?

Religions are all sick in their essence. That is not good to watch, because the principle of their approaches has all been good, but the

power games of the higher echelons ... the hunger for power was the reason that this body of thought has changed and with that, created and still does create negativity. The principle that the masculine is suppressing the feminine in these religions is a fact that I cannot but look at with concern, because I see that the feminine energy cannot be at peace, which is its nature, but instead has to compete with the masculine energy and that is wrong. The war of the sexes, as you call it, is a result of the power games of the mighty.

What can you do about this?

That is a good question; I am doing what I can over here but I do not know how effective this is ...

Once in a ritual, I experienced words as veritable energy gestalts. Can you explain to me and to the people in your words what exactly happens when people speak?

That is a beautiful question, Sylvia ... the energy of words is like energy that comes to life. You create life in the energy space. That is very, very important. People who think that what they say is of no consequence still have not understood what they are doing. Words are beings and they continue to exist until they are changed into another form. But that can only happen through transformation, and if you do not know what it is that you have to transform, you cannot do this. This is also the main reason for all the hurtful barbs that I experienced when I was a human being.

Is there something you miss about being incarnated?

∞

Perhaps the intoxicating moments when I was with my beloved. It truly is very beautiful to experience this type of perception, but I do not really want to look in that direction; it is too beautiful here.

Is there something you would like to impart to the people who come to Abadiânia?

Yes, with pleasure. The people come here in order to heal, but many forget what healing actually means. Healing is the balancing of the energies that you have created; that means that you have to
1. Find out what caused them,
2. Enter into the process and
3. Transmute this energy.
The tools for all of these steps are all provided here, we direct you into the queue that will be the next one for you and then we go inside you and transform the energies if you are ready. That is all.

203

What is the biggest mistake that the people tend to make over here?

They do not rest enough, they talk constantly, they constantly talk and that is costing them a lot of energy. They will not regenerate in this way. It is silence that holds the energy; this is how all the energy can be utilized for the healing. This is important.
I would strongly advise them to go into absolute silence already in the hall, or to remain silent as the case may be. Everyone can pray in silence, you do not need a stage for this. It is alright to pray loudly but all the action around these prayers, all this explaining is not good. It demands attention and completely distracts you from the essence of the devotion that is supposed to happen here.

Do you also perceive all of the shining orbs?

Yes, they are everywhere. The orbs are friends; we love them.

Can you communicate with then?

Yes. All energy is conscious; you know that.

What makes you sad when you treat people here in Abadiânia?

It makes me sad when I realise that many a person does not really want to heal, and I ask myself why he has travelled so far.

What makes you joyful?

204

The blossoming of the cloud.

When you come into your own power as a human being, you also recognize negativity. On the one hand, you want to help, on the other hand you need to protect yourself from things like that; how is this supposed to work? How should we deal with this, that there are so many things at once, that we can create the positive and the negative and that they are both here at the same time?

The question is not how many forms there are; the question is what you yourself are like. The answer to your question is that where there is a yes, there is a yes; where there is a no, there is a no. Energy does not lie. Energy is energy, and if you can read it, you are being guided by cosmic harmony and you will not experience or create disharmony.

And how can you translate this into the world of business, of professional life?

> *That is very easy, the people who use you are not friends; these energies when looked at from a distance are not in devotion. Devotion, surrender, is for all those who are loving and act lovingly. That is all.*
>
> *The teachings of love are manifold; I would like to teach you, but I will need a lot of time for this. Please continue to contact me and we will communicate about this further.*

Would you like to impart one lesson to us today?

> *The first lesson of love is trust. Love is like a force that needs trust. Love cannot exist without trust. That is essential.*

205

So this means when we tell the people to trust more, that at the same time this means love more?

> *Yes.*

But what about the people who have been betrayed because they have placed their trust in someone?

> *That is a different form of love. I am talking about the love that is inherent in everything, love as the force of existence. This love is only possible where there is trust, and I mean trust in life!*

What do we tell those who have been betrayed?

The people who have been betrayed will find their power once more in the love that I mean, the love of existence.

Yes, but many are looking for this love only among other people...

Yes, that is right, but love is much more multifaceted, it is not just the love for another human being. That is quite another thing and most often just attraction, not love in the sense which I mean. Love between two people is very rarely in the power that I call true cosmic love. Love between people is usually guided by ego and therefore cannot be open and expansive.

I thank you very much for the wonderful messages!

I thank you.

Jesus

We all know the historical figure of Jesus Christ and the impulses he gave to our spiritual development. Once or twice before, I have had the privilege to talk to the energy that people invoke by the name of Jesus. Communication with this energy gestalt has a very special quality. His energy is full of love but there is also a deep sadness. I always sense this sadness when I contact him and it makes me weep a lot. His energy is rather august, very highly vibrating and surrounded by an enormous layer of protection. It is not easy to get through to him and he is very reticent in his answers. Even before I contacted him the first time, I was told by the Wise Brotherhood to abstain from asking him about previous lives or his transitions but instead to concentrate on my other questions.

This is why for this book I have tried to keep my questions brief and to the point.

Interview

I am requesting an interview with the entity that the people invoke as Jesus Christ.

Hello, I am ready.

I have met several entities now that all work in your name in order to help the people – can you perceive them?

Very faintly; I am on a different level from them and I cannot as yet perceive their energy very clearly – but that could change. I just need to concentrate upon them.

Does the name of Dom Ignacio de Loyola mean anything to you?

Yes.

What exactly is your relationship with him?

This entity has been especially devoted to me in his prayer, which has been very connecting. I therefore began to take him into my guidance. This entity's energy is well known to me; it is true.

And have you ever met with him on the spiritual planes?

No, he is on another level and I do not want to go there because the vibrations there are lower and I need the high energy here on this level.

∞

But you know that he, like yourself, once worked on earth and that he did much of what he did in your name?

Yes.

I am currently in a place called Abadiânia, where Dom Ignacio has established an institution with the help of a human being who has dedicated his life to helping people – do you know of this?

Yes, the idea to establish such an institution was mine.

That means that Dom Ignacio received the impulse from you?

Yes.

Did you know of this place already?

Yes, I knew it because I can sense the energy on the surface of the earth from here, but I did not know what Dom Ignacio would make of it with his energy.

Together with King Solomon he has found a way to incorporate into a human being in order to help, did you know that?

Yes.

And you observed all that?

Yes, but observing these impulses is different from directing one's full attention to the place.

∞

Dear Jesus, would you like to leave a message for mankind in this place?

The message I have for the people is that my thoughts are always with them. My life's experience was very painful, but whenever a human being took love into their heart, I was happy again. If they only lived one day in love, then they have truly lived. If there was just one moment that brought a smile to their face, that moment has not been lost. Love must be nurtured especially carefully. It is like a flower, for when the buds open, they also wither and need to be reborn; there is also a death and rebirth in this energy, the suffering arises from this lovelessness or rather weakness of love. It is attention that sets the direction, not inattention!

But love never dies in the cosmos…

That is true, but it must be nurtured in the human awareness.

And this is the reason why you have brought the prayer and all that into the world, right?

Yes.

From which level are you talking to me?

From the sixth level, but I am in a special area.

Would you like to leave another message for the people today?

No.

∞

Then I will transmit your message to the people, I thank you very much for this.

That is well; I thank you.

Bezerra de Menezes

His full name is Adolfo Bezerra de Menezes Cavalcanti. He was born on August 29, 1831 in what was then called Freguesia do Riacho do Sangue, today the town of Jaguaretama in the State of Ceara, Brazil. He was a monk, teacher, doctor, service member, politician, businessman and author.

Bezerra's father was very wealthy, but he bequeathed all his money to charity, leaving his son a legacy of respectability and integrity. Consequently, Bezerra de Menezes had to endure periods of material poverty, but he was always ready to give all that he had to the poor. He had received a Catholic baptism but later in life converted to spiritualism after reading Allan Kardec's "The Spirits Book".

It is worth mentioning an incident that happened at the time that Bezerra was reading medicine. He had been in dire straits financially and desperately needed 50.000 Röis, the Brazilian currency at the time, in order to pay off various debts, including the rent for his room (he was facing eviction). In his desperation, he turned to God for help. A few days later, a personable and well-educated young man knocked on his door, professing to be in need of a mathematics teacher. Bezerra strongly disliked this subject but owing to his desperation and the young man's insistence he reluctantly accepted an advance payment of 50.000 Röis. He paid off his debts and studied hard in order to prepare for his lessons. But the young man never reappeared. Many years later during a seance, he was asked to dedicate more time to helping people spiritually. When Bezerra protested that he would not be able to do so as he was obliged to work in order to support himself, the spirit of Saint Augustine manifested before him, saying: "We will help you by sending new students of mathematics, should you need them."

A noteworthy quote by Bezzerra:
"A doctor neither has the right to finish a meal nor to ask whether it is far or near when a person in need is knocking at his door. He who does not bestir himself because he is entertaining company, is too busy, too tired or because it is too late at night; or who demands to be sent transport by someone who is barely able to pay for the medicine, or who tells someone weeping at his door to go to someone else is not a doctor but a peddler of medicine."

Owing to Bezerra's dedication to his work and to his enduring charity, he was called "the doctor of the poor". For many years, he was president of the Spiritualist Society of Brazil (Federação Espírita Brasileira), which also earned him the moniker "the Brazilian Kardec." He died on April 11, 1900.

(Source: Spiritual Healing, Ismar E. Garcia)

Interview

I now call the energy known to the people as Bezerra de Menezes. Dear Bezerra, I would like to contact you because you are linked to the energy entities that work in Abadiânia.

That is right.

Can you tell me a little about who you are and where you come from?

That is not necessary.

Could you try anyway to tell me about your reason for doing what you do? Could you tell me a little bit about your lifetime?

Yes.

I would like to know which were the most wonderful moments of your last lifetime.

I was very rich as a young man because my father carried much wealth, but it was not given into my hands when he died, so instead I started a new life. The people needed help and I have tried in my own way to supply this, but I was a captive of matter.

What happened to change that?

This is known.

∞

You mean the story about the student of mathematics?

No, the story that is known about how the Masters appeared before me.

Would you like to tell me more about it?

This is inconsequential. At the time, I was in a state of mind that made me very desperate; I wanted and needed to choose what to do with my life. Then I sensed the presence of an entity that I subsequently also saw.

And how did you see it?

The energy of this entity was very bright and I perceived it as warm. That was very beautiful and this moment was the best moment of that time.

215

And were there other beautiful moments?

Yes, then I began to walk the path of healing the people and my soul. Both are connected to each other. We are all healing while healing other people.

What made you most happy?

That I was able to really help some people because I could transmit many messages to them and give them many impulses that turned out to be helpful. But of course, I also experienced the downside of this work, as I did not always receive thanks for it. That is all right, however, I am past that now.

Would you like to tell me about your transition into the other world?

With pleasure: The energy that I became was the new form. This began when I shed the human form and began to perceive new things. My perception gradually changed and I became brighter and brighter. I flew over the clouds and the trees, I was happy in this feeling; that was beautiful. Then I arrived at the level of the shining orbs and they escorted me to the level of the Masters. This is where I now dwell.

So you are on the third level?

Yes.

You were talking through Chico and in this could impart on Joao where he was to go to do his work, is that right?

Yes.

How did you receive this information?

I received the information from this perception in the intermediary world. There, I perceived the earth's energy. It was very bright and clear in that place, I remembered this and also how he could work there.

How exactly did that happen?

I saw the energy of the place and its connection to the world of the shining orbs; this was like a channel in my perception. Because I had arrived at the level of the shining orbs, I knew that this was a good thing and I therefore wanted Joao to be able to work there in that energy. That was right, I believe.

Yes, you did that exactly right. Thank you for this many times. Were you afraid in your state of transition?

No... Fear is not a force known to us who have neither body nor ego.

How do you work now, as a Master?

That is easy to say; I Am. I just am and when I am called, I am there.

217

That means that you work as a Master.

Yes.

Did you ever believe that one day you would work as a Master in the cosmos?

(Smiles) Very funny question; energy is energy, we can transform it, but in principle, the potential has already been set. I was always a Master energy.

Is there a special subject that people can invoke you about?

I can obtain information that has a bearing on other subjects. It depends on the question.

And do you have a special subject about which you are best able to obtain and pass on information?

The soul in its perception of lack.

What does this look like?

The soul that perceives lack is not connected with the real energy. This creates the feeling of loneliness and loss; and so it is easy to help them. We send them energy when they ask for it.

Who is "we"?

The other Masters.

Can you see how Joao and the other entities work?

I see what happens in Abadiânia but I cannot see the other entities, they are on another level (author's note: the fourth level). The shining orbs really make good progress but I also see how they often work in vain. Of course this is too sweeping a statement, but I think you know what I mean.

Yes, I understand. Would you like to leave a message for the people?

The energy of this place is unique in the whole world. I ask the people to bear this in mind and not to waste it in futile conversa-

tions amongst each other. The energy is very important in order to heal, therefore it is helpful for the people to walk and remain in silence. This is the essence of the healing process.

And would you like to also leave a message for those who do not succeed in healing themselves?

That is not my work.

Would you like to reincarnate on earth?

No, I abhor it. This mode of being.

Would you like to pass on anything else?

Very few would understand it. But I will try anyway.

Please proceed.

The soul's energy is not a perpetuum mobile. Although we can transmute this energy further, the actual source is the source and it is the soul's task to recognize the connection with the source, to find it, to strengthen it and to maintain it. This is exclusively the responsibility of the person. This is the essence of my message. I do not need to say more. This is the essence.

You seem very determined and serious; is there a reason for this?

I did not know that, it just is my way...

I read that you lived around the turn of the 18th/19th century – was this your way of communication at the time?

I do not know what you mean – but yes, we communicated like that.

No, don't worry, I did not mean to judge, I just wanted to be able to categorize it, because every entity has a very individual style of communication and in comparison to the others, you seem rather formal and abrupt.

I thank you very much for your devotion and your information. I wish you a beautiful moment...

You have said this well, because truly, everything here is but a moment, but I know what you mean. I thank you as well.

220

Sister Sheila

Sister Sheila was born in Germany. Originally, she trained as a nurse. During World War 2, she predominantly looked after casualties of war. She died in July or August 1943 during an air raid.

It is also known that in an earlier incarnation, she was Jeanne-Françoise Fremiot, born in France on January 28, 1572 and died in Dijon on December 13, 1641. During her French existence, she had dedicated her life to social aid and was canonized in 1767 as Saint Jeanne de Chantal. The spiritual work of the entity called Sister Sheila consists of treating the sick and infirm. Her presence is accompanied by a specific fragrance.

(Source: Spiritual Healing, Ismar E. Garcia)

Interview

Dear entity known by the people as Sister Sheila. I hope I pronounce your name correctly.

It is pronounced correctly. You said it correctly.

I am happy to make your acquaintance.

And I, yours.

Sister Sheila, you are a very delicate and very slow energy. I would like to get to know you better now.

With pleasure.

I would like to let you choose which of your lives you would like to talk about.

This is truly a nice idea. I choose the life in France because after that, I experienced only misery during the war. That is not worth mentioning.

Then please tell me, what was your life in France like?

I grew up in a very protected environment as a child. My parents love was very great and I was always protected, but one day I lost both parents though an illness. That was very sad. I did not know what to do and went to the monastery nearby. I grew up there and

was able to regain the protection that I had lost as a child. At the same time, I learned much about healing and was able to alleviate much suffering working as a doctor. Mine was the knowledge of the nuns, but I loved people and I always loved to live in readiness to help.

So you did not have children?

No.

Married?

No, mine was the love of God.

Were there beautiful moments in your life?

223

There were many; the healings that we performed were always very gladdening. This is the feeling I remember to this day.

And what made you sad?

The people who did not want to listen, it was a mystery to me that people would ask on the one hand and then not listen to the answer on the other hand. I had to learn to accept that. This is the way of humans, after all.

And then you died in the monastery.

Yes, I did, but I was not alone. The many sisters were with me.

∞

Would you like to talk about your passing?

With pleasure. I was in that room which was my cell and I began to feel the detachment from my body because it was getting colder and colder. That was a little creepy in a way because I so loved the warmth, but I was conscious and at the same time, I felt that I was getting colder and colder.

Then my perception began to change even more. I went into a different state of being. I did perceive the sisters around me but in a different way. I saw their energy that was around me but I did not see their faces. Then I went on to a higher level. There, again, I was together with others. It was bright there and I liked it very much. Then my energy started to move again onto a higher level. Suddenly, I was in a world full of energy lights. Those were the shining orbs that I saw.

224

Did it occur to you that these orbs could be angels?

No, that was the crazy thing. All my life, I had prayed to the angels especially and then, when I was with them, I did not recognize them (she laughs).

And what happened next?

Then I went onto the next level, the level of the Masters. Over there, I was in contact with many other beings and we communicated. This level has been my place until this day, as you would say, although "today" would not be the right term, but I think that you understand what I mean.

Yes, I do. So you are on the third level, on the level of the Masters.

Yes.

And still you come to Abadiânia from time to time in order to work here. How did this come to pass?

That is a funny story. I was on this level of the Masters and saw how energy was flowing from the entity that you call Dom Ignacio to the human beings. You have to imagine this like a channel; this is the way I perceived this. It had its source on another level but worked through our level. I observed this attentively and it made me curious. Then I wanted to talk to him about it, but he was above me and I could not get there and therefore I did not know what to do. Then Dom Ignacio began to hear my calling and went to me, and he explained to me what he was doing. That was very interesting and I wanted to do this as well. Then he explained to me how I could do this and I followed him. I am not really able to enter Joao's body but I like being connected to the place and this is how I participate.

225

Oh, I see, you participate in the operations by giving your energy?

Yes.

Did you ever incorporate in Joao?

...It was an attempt... his energy is better suited to male energy. Even when we are genderless, it is still better to differentiate between the qualities. This is what I mean to say... it is not really the gender, but there are no other words for this in your world. The

souls have retained characteristics from their previous lives and mine is feminine and soft. This also makes my energy rather feminine and soft. Because of this, I do not find it as easy to go into him as the penetrating force of the male human energy is accustomed to doing. This is an experience shared by entities whose last lives were lived in the male power.

(Author's note: She says this with a light smirk.)

But now you are genderless?

Yes.

How do you perceive your level now?

226

The level is wide open and beautiful. The landscape is full of flowers and peaceful areas. This makes it very pleasant to be here.

Would you like to return to earth?

No, this suffering and the pain, the restless way of the humans is too much for me, I only did the last life because I really wanted to help.
Now I have found the right form of existence.

Is there something that makes you especially happy in your work here?

To observe the people when they are truly healing, that is really wonderful.

∞

And what makes you very sad?

The people when they do not wish to heal; it is a mystery to me. The people are confused.

Do you perform visual operations?

No. I like to participate in the energetic operations; I am more of an accompanying presence.

Do you perceive all the shining orbs here?

Yes, of course.

And you now understand that those orbs represent angels in the nomen-clature of the people?

I was not aware that these orbs were supposed to be the angels but I know now why you communicate it like this in your world. The orbs fly very speedily and they are soft and loving, that is the same power that is also ascribed to angels.

Dear Sheila, if you like you can give me a message to the people and I will write it down.

Oh, I would like to do this very much. You tell them please that we are always with them. The separation that people feel is not a separation; it is just a distorted perception. We are all connected to each other, even when you are in a body which is by its nature less able to sense that, but it is the truth.

∞

Do you have a favourite place in the *Casa*?

> *The Chapel. There are many shining orbs there and I like the energy of the place. There are fewer people there and it is so quiet.*

How do you perceive Abadiânia?

> *This place is magical.*

I have one more question, about the church and how you perceive it from your current perspective. As a servant of the church, what do you say about this?

> *I do not wish to comment on that, it makes me uncomfortable. The church as you experience it is not what I have learned and experienced. The power of the mighty in the church is the contamination of the message.*

228

Well, they are currently trying very hard to rectify that?

> *They will only succeed if they stop their power games and no longer suppress the female energy in the sense of denying it equal status in their messages.*

May I ask you about other religions?

> *It is similar there. There are all vast structures there but the power games are a problem with all of them. Wherever the people are being manipulated through power, the message is distorted and the intention void.*

What would be the correct form of religion, what would you change?

I would bring love as the only message to humanity. The method does not matter, but it has to be in a loving way.

Dear Sheila, would you say anything else to the people?

No.

Then I thank you for your delicate being and the great information, your joy and your smile.

I thank you as well, until another time.

229

Euripides Barsanulfo

Euripedes Barsanulfo was born on May 1, 1880 in Sacramento, Minas Gerais, Brazil. He was enormously intelligent and therefore began to teach from an early age, having been asked by his teachers to assist in instructing his fellow pupils. He had an obvious talent for leadership and later went on to act as secretary of the Daughters of Charity of Saint Vincent de Paul. Although an autodidact, he taught several subjects and worked as a journalist and politician.

Euripedes Barsanulfo learned about the teachings of Allan Kardec through an uncle. He read about it extensively and then converted to spiritualism. The lack of understanding on the part of his friends and family concerning spiritualism brought him much sadness. He was audacious enough to include this subject in his teaching activities, which led to strong opposition against him. He lost many students who were taken out of the school by their incensed parents.

Traumatized by persecution and a general lack of understanding, he withdrew from his professional activities, seeking healing and rest. During that time, Barsanulfo's latent spiritual talents came to the surface, especially the gift to administer healing. One of the first people who benefitted from this newly found gift of healing was his own mother. Soon, the city of Sacramento became a place of pilgrimage for people seeking relief from physical and psychological afflictions. Euripedes Barsanulfo became a devoted healer, exercising his gift with joy and dedication.

As his spiritual activities increased, he felt the need to spread the new doctrine in order to raise the number of devotees. With the help of some family members and friends he founded the Grupo Espírita Esperança e Caridade (The Spiritual Centre of Hope and Charity).

Physically, he was of weak constitution, but as he was a personable man, there were many ladies interested in marriage. But Euripedes declared that he was unable to do so, being already "married to poverty".

He founded the College Allan Kardec in 1907. It soon gained the reputation of a centre of learning in the region and later on in all of Brazil. Soon, all available places for the study programme tended to be booked out on the first day of enrolment. But when the Spanish influenza broke out in the second decade of the 20th century, the institute was forced to close its doors for a while. Barsanulfo spent all his energy on helping the victims of the influenza and to help their frequently impoverished relatives.

One day, Euripedes Barsanulfo fell into a trance while teaching. When he came to he related details of the Versailles Meeting that was to take place in France after the end of World War 1. He was able to name the participants and the exact time of day.

Barsanulfo was not interested in a confrontation with official religion, but he humbly accepted the challenge to a public debate extended by a member of the Catholic Church. He acquitted himself brilliantly in every respect, preaching love, tolerance and charity. This only served to raise him in public estimation. The same thing happened when he was taken to court on one occasion; the case was later dropped.

Exhausted by his strenuous work, Euripedes Barsanulfo died on November 1, 1918, surrounded by family, friends and admirers.

(Source: Spiritual Healing, Ismar E. Garcia)

Interview

I call the entity known to the people as Euripedes Barsanulfo.

Dear Euripedes, I am happy to be able to talk with you; how are you?

I have been very weak but now I am very well.

From which level are you talking to me?

From the fourth level.

I would like to get to know you better: your personality, your work. I have heard that you incorporate into Joao from time to time. I have also read how much of a multi-talent you were. Let us start with your last lifetime. How did you experience that time in all these functions?

All of that was a little too banal for my liking. The people needed the guidance. They handed it to me without really asking me first.

Was there a special moment you remember fondly?

The encounter with a friend of the spiritualist teachings.

What fascinated you most about them?

The expansion.

How had you perceived life up to that point?

The people were mysterious beings to me because I protected their perceptions but in some cases they hurt me for this.

What happened then, after you met this person?

The spiritualist teachings required a lot of attention and I meditated a lot, but despite this I also continued to work as a teacher.

What was it like to juggle teaching and studying?

That was very connecting. I have connected the teachings of the human beings with the teaching of spiritualism. That was a great joy for me; I was able to bring expansion into the constriction in this way.

But I also heard that some of your students turned away from you because of this?

This was not a real threat because they came back, as soon as these children could make their own decisions.

What happened then?

These teachings brought even more benefits. One day I awoke and a special kind of energy was coursing through me. It was like a connection to a level that I had not known before. This energy flowed through my hands.

How did you notice that?

I noticed that because my hands became very hot. From then on, they were always hot but there were moments when I was distracted; then I did not feel this power so strongly.

And what happened then?

Then I was able to release many blockages inside my mother. That was her healing.

And then?

This made the rounds in the land and this gift was the reason why more and more people came to me. I began to develop it and then I let go of my work as a teacher and just did the healings.

234

How did you perceive the people at that time?

The people needed help; I wanted to help them.

And what happened then?

Then the Spanish influenza came and I had to heal much. The people needed strength and I had a lot of strength and so I tried to pass this on to them.
The Spanish influenza required all my attention and I lost a lot of strength through that. That was not good. That is why I had to allow the energy inside me to expire until I myself was no longer able to live.

But then you gave so much that in the end you had nothing left for yourself; is this wise?

That was not the question; it was my task to give the energy to the people, not how long and where.

Are you satisfied with your actions?

Yes.

How were you able to perceive whether this helped the people?

The people to whom I gave this energy became more and more connected and this connection was the reason why they healed, because the energy was flowing again and the healing process had started inside them.

235

Then you died very young.

Yes.

Are you sad about that?

No, my work is done.

Was it your soul's task to come and help during the Spanish influenza?

No, my soul's task was to pass on the knowledge and to create the connections.

Then when you died, you were happy?

Yes.

Would you like to talk about your passing?

Yes, the first thing I perceived was the connection that I had to the other levels. That was like a ladder that showed itself to me. Then I began my journey through time. I saw the people; how they lost this energy inside themselves and then went to these wars. That was very sad. Then I went into the level of the deceased. There, it was very bright and I was happy there, but I knew that this was not my home. Then I went on to another level owing to a movement in the region of my heart. Then I was with the angels. I perceived them as entities full of light, which up to this day I would rather describe as shining orbs but that is of no consequence. Then I was a little intoxicated and stayed there for a while.

What did you do there?

I just stayed there and observed.

And then?

Then I became bored and I wanted to move on; this is why I went up to the next level, the level of the Masters. There were many of my friends there that I had known in other lifetimes. These energies were waiting for me and I was very happy to see them again. There we communicated and lived happily together. Then there came a moment when I knew that I wanted to move on because my task in these levels was more than just to be. So I went into the next level. There, I met with the Masters and allied myself to them. These en-

ergies vibrated even higher and were even purer than the others. I liked that very much. Then I saw how Dom Ignacio was taking care of this ladder into the other level and I wanted to participate. That is why I went over there and I observed it and very soon I went with him into the descending function that these entities take on.

And then you incorporated in Joao?

Yes.

What was that like for you?

The power that is in him is unique. He is soft and powerful at the same time. This is interesting to observe. Still I wanted to know what it is like to be inside him, that is why I went into his body. That was very constricted.

237

How did you perceive the people through Joao?

This perception was new to me, because suddenly I saw that they carried a type of energy inside them which I was able to read. This is like looking at a book that had been empty up to this point and suddenly you see the letters. That is a very interesting perception. Some people are very pure and they just need strength, the others are very contaminated and need to be cleansed. Still others are hungry for love and need attention, which we can give them, but I know that we will not be able to help them.

And then?

Then I began my work here and I was very happy doing that.

Do you also perform visible operations?

No.

Are you seldom inside Joao or why do I hear more about other entities incorporating into him?

I prefer to work from the other level because Joao's body is too constricted for my liking. I do not like this feeling, this is why I prefer to stay on the other level and participate in the invisible operations.

Is there something that makes you sad as you perform these operations?

238

That many do not wish to heal because they keep holding on to old blockages.

Is there something that makes you very happy when you do this?

Yes, the people who heal; some of them need a lot of time, but you can see how they flourish; the others do not need as much time and start healing immediately. That is always very beautiful to watch.

How do you perceive this?

This is like a flower that opens...

Would you give to leave a message for the people who come here to

∞

Abadiânia?

*Yes, with pleasure, you can tell them that I am always very happy
when they come here. Love is the only key, the only power we
move over here, and the people can unfold their love even more
if they open their hearts. This is very important to me. The hearts
are the key to healing.*

Would you like to say something about the church?

*Yes, the church in this form is the worst that could have happened
to the people, because the idea is still good but the implementa-
tion is not right. This is like taking the wrong road to the right des-
tination.*

If you like, you can expand on that. 239

*You have to tell them that the narrowness of the church will not
bring them the healing that they desire. They will find their healing in the expansion of the soul, this is why it is up to everyone how
much of the church's teaching they accept or not. But in principle,
this is not a healthy association.*

Why is it not healthy in your eyes?

*I do not know, in my opinion it is because of the many people who
are so sick in spirit but sit there and teach. That is not good, because a sick spirit cannot teach healthy things.*

What do you say to the other religions on our planet, do they have

∞

similar problems?

Yes, in all religions it is not expansion that they teach, even when they are convinced that they do. But their structures prevent that. Then it is the female energy they suppress and with that, the experience of wholeness. This again is a sick attitude. Then it is the joy they take away from the people. There is no religion that teaches that joy and love are the most important parameters of being human. It is a mystery to me how such simple truths are not being communicated. These are the most important points that I would criticize. It would be very good if you could communicate that.

With pleasure. Did you already see it like that during your life?

No, I just felt that something was not right and I turned away from these things, but still I did not know exactly how to name it or what lay at the bottom of the problem.

How did you reach your current conclusion?

They possess no heart energy when they are captured by this belief. This is a real correlation, because the church's doctrines profess to be all about heart energy but they actually achieve the contrary. The hearts of the people become rough and closed, not alive and open.

Is this due to all the church's interdictions, commandments and rules?

Yes, interdictions are rules and rules create a structure and a structure can constrict.

Would you like to reincarnate as a human being once more?

No, up to this point, I have not felt the urge; the way I can work here is the only right way for me, because I do not have to allow myself to get hurt and I still can give love. The need to create connections goes without saying, but I would still prefer to do it in this form.

But if all the people who want to give love chose not to return to earth, that would not be good either, would it?

Yes, it would be perfectly all right; especially in places like Abadiânia and with people like Joao we are able to achieve more than if we were incarnate.

Do you have a favourite place in the *Casa*?

241

No.

Can you perceive the shining orbs?

Yes, of course. This is beautiful, they are so fine and nice to look at, and full of love, that is wonderful to look at time and time again. The shining orbs are bright and sometimes a little colourful.

Why do you think that some of them are coloured?

That is when they carry some energy inside them that needs to be transformed.

Then I have no more questions for now; would you like to add something?

No, it was very nice to talk to you.

See you soon.

See you soon.

Amor

I read in Ismar E. Garcia's book *Spiritual Healing* that there is also an entity called "Amor". Because I am very inquisitive I also tried to establish contact with this entity. I succeeded relatively quickly.
This energy is very highly elevated and very, very delicate.

Interview

I'm very curious as to who is behind the name of Amor. Dear entity named Amor, is this your real name or is it a name given to you by humans?

My name is Amor because my energy is the embodiment of love.

Why did you reveal yourself to mankind under this name?

Because I am the power of love and because this word in this language is understood by every human being.

(Author's note: Amor is Latin for love.)

Were you ever a human being?

No.

From which level are you talking to me?

You cannot describe the level from which I speak. You do not know it yet.

Then I am the happier that I am allowed to meet you today because this way, I can expand my own energy.

You have been here before, but not whilst you were working in the body in which you are now.

What exactly am I to call you? Entity; entity of power; Amor?

Amor is exactly right. Amor.

The entities that incorporate into Joao usually come from the third, fourth and fifth level. Can you give us a brief description of where you are in the cosmos?

I am part of the level of transformation which you call the last level. The Wise Brotherhood is below my state of being.

Oh; so you are in the seventh level?

The last level and the first level of form. Then there is only the source itself.

245

So you have a form?

It is possible for me to animate a body but not a human body. The energy is too high, but I can concentrate on bringing this power into a form, which can then go into a body like the entities do with Joao.

There, where you are, are there many other entities?

No, this level is empty because there are no forms here.

To whom or to what do I speak then, when I am speaking into form-lessness?

You are speaking to the power of love.

How big is this power, if you wanted to describe it?

You cannot think in terms of form here; this is not possible. Form does not exist here, not even the oval form of the entities.

How do you perceive me?

You are pure energy inside a bubble of light and you are visiting me on this level. I perceive your energy but not your shape as a human being.

So you have no eyes?

246

No, I am pure consciousness.

How did you get to Ignacio and Joao?

The energy of these entities is very industrious. They are very eager. I felt this power and I wanted to know where it comes from. This is why I went to the level of the masters, [from] where they act, and observed how they work.

Were you able to communicate with them?

Yes, this was possible. I would have been able to communicate with them, but they did not perceive me.

Because you have no form?

Yes.

And how did it happen that you then went into the body of Joao?

I just did it. I bundled the energy and I went into a form. This form then visited Joao and his shining orbs. Then I went inside him and tried to understand the human beings.

And? What was that like?

The experience was very intense, because until then I did not know the nature of the human beings who are not living in love; I have experienced it there what it is like to live without love.

What did this look like to you?

247

The power of the human beings was just cold and close to existence.

What do you mean, close to existence?

The energy was just enough to animate the organism, but not enough to attain awareness.

And how did you perceive the energy?

The energy bodies of the people were very dark and I have found little love inside them, especially in their hearts, but we have been able to help many and to open their hearts.

∞

What was that like for you?

That was very beautiful to watch, but I did not wish to assume this form any longer, it was too constricted for me. The way "I am" now is more appropriate for me.

So you do not plan to incorporate into Joao any more?

I do not know yet.

You now have the possibility to leave a message for the people, Amor.

The people are connected to the power of love and can increase this power. This is an integral part of life. Increasing this power. But many do not know this yet and therefore they do not live it. The people have to learn that they are themselves responsible for their destiny and their creations. The power can only increase if they wish it and act accordingly. The power will never grow if the people expect this without awareness. The power will diminish if the people do not live love!

248

Dear Amor, it was a great pleasure to have spoken with you.

Thank you for your work.

Emanuel

The entity of Emanuel is known predominantly by the fact that he was the spiritual mentor of Chico Xavier. It is also known that in a previous lifetime, he was the proud Roman senator Publius Lentulus, who had lived in luxury and debauchery by the grace of Julius Cesar. He was married to Livia, whose execution he was forced to watch from the gallery. She died because she had converted to Christianity. Lentulus himself died in Pompeii in 79 BC when Vesuvius erupted.

In order to atone for his sins he reincarnated 50 years later as the slave Nestorio, who together with other Christians of all ages was devoured by wild beasts in the Roman arena to serve as entertainment for the Roman public.

About 150 years later he walked on earth as the Roman patrician Quinto Varro who assumed the identity of an old preacher named Corvino in order to escape an attempt on his life. He was sentenced to death by beheading but this sentence was later converted to a slow death in the dungeons.

Many centuries passed, and in the year of 1517 he reincarnated in Portugal as the man who was to become Padre Manuel da Nobrega, an important figure in the Society of Christ founded by Ignacio de Loyola. He played an important part in the history of Brazil including the founding of the College of Piratininga, the cradle of the huge metropolis of São Paulo. He died of tuberculosis at the age of 53 in Rio de Janeiro.

Manuel da Nobrega used to write his name as Ermano da Nobrega (= *brother* Manuel); hence the name of the entity is given as *Emanuel.*

(Source: Spiritual Healing, Ismar E. Garcia)

∞

Interview

I now ask the energy known to the people as Emanuel to emerge so that I may communicate with it.

Dear Emanuel, how are you; there are tears coming to my eyes?

You are very sensitive; these tears are a part of my soul.

What do you wish to be called?

Emanuel.

I would like to ask you a few questions as I have done with all the other entities that are active here in Abadiânia. Is it true that you are also working here?

(Hesitantly) ... yes, I am here as well, but less so than the others.

Dear Emanuel, please tell me a bit about yourself; what moves you, what touches you. What was the path of your soul? I have read about several of your previous lives, were these written down correctly?

Yes.

Which stations on your path would you like to talk to me about?

Travelling in time is not really important to me, but the path of the soul is.

∞

I understand that, but the people can understand you better when you tell them about your lives.

It is especially difficult for me to put these stations back into words. You can do this better.

Yes, but I need your help in order to do this. Can you talk about these lives?

No, it is not necessary.

Please tell me, where are you now?

I am now on the fourth level and I am with the other Masters.

252   What do you do there?

I pray.

I did not know that entities prayed as well?

You are funny, why shouldn't we pray...

Well, normally the people pray into the spiritual world, but you are in the spiritual world; so to whom are you speaking?

To God, of course.

And why do you pray so much?

The energy that I feel when doing this, it is so healing, I need this.

Would you like to talk to the people about your transitions?

No, that is not appropriate.

Then please describe to me how you found your way into the Casa, or rather, how did you find Dom Ignacio on your level and how did you perceive him?

The Casa had always been one of the ideas that Ignacio had during his life and perhaps even before this, but I have learnt about this for the first time when I was with him. This time (author's note: as a human being and a friend of Dom Ignacio) was very important because I could feel how connected he was.

253

How did you perceive him as a human being, in his life time?

The energy inside him was very pure and I always liked it when he spoke. This power and this love were unique.

What happened then? Did you meet him again by coincidence, when you were no longer a human being and he was no longer a human being?

The energy of the human being does not only exist when it is in a body, but when the energy leaves the body, it continues to exist. This is the reason why in my search for healing I searched again and again for the energy of Ignacio; in this incarnation, which was my last, and when I then died, I wanted all the more to find my way to his home.

∞

Do you mean by this that Ignacio's energy served as a kind of homing beacon that could lead you to where you wanted to go, even before and especially after your death?

The cleansing of my soul was especially important in this process. I could not reach him as long as I was still contaminated. The power of the soul is not very great when it is contaminated.

And after your last life you have been purified enough to be able to reach him?

That is correct, I was the purity that was needed in order to get to his level, the level of the Masters of the Qualities.

And what was that like for you?

That was very nice, I greeted him like a brother. My soul was danc-ing with joy because I knew that I had cleansed a large part of my energy and I was back with him. It was like a homecoming for me.

And then?

Then I observed how he worked. I have seen the ladder that is lead-ing down into the Casa, and I saw how he was going into Joao's body; I wanted to be able to do this as well, and then I learned it.

What was that like when you did it for the first time?

It was fascinating, I was still in the perception of the spiritual be-ings, but I was in a human body. That is very constructive.

And what did you perceive?

The first times were very frightening because I felt very constricted, but I got used to it. Then it began to be easier and easier; and if I want to do it now, it is easier.

How did you perceive the people in comparison to when you were human yourself?

The energy of the people is changeable and I have seen these many forms of energy inside them. It was very exciting to receive these colours and this information.

How can I visualise that? How do you learn about the cause of an illness?

It is information that I read.

So you see the organ or the meridian that is not in energetic balance and this is then the cause of the illness, right?

That is correct.

But some people have many organs which are out of balance, haven't they?

Unfortunately this is often the case, yes. The people have one peculiarity: They learn little about their energy and on top of this, on top of the fact that they do not know anything about it, they keep on destroying it. That is unbelievable.

Oh, unfortunately we do not learn this in school, you must not be angry with them.

I know that. There is still much hope in me that books like yours or by people like you can change this.

What makes you sad when you are healing here through Joao?

Having to realise that not all of the people want to walk the path of healing. Most of them want attention.

Are there really so many who only want attention?

Yes, unfortunately there are very many.

According to your perception, how many people out of a hundred only want attention through their illness, and how many want to really heal their illness?

50 people out of a hundred only want attention.

And what makes you very happy?

To observe the people when they are healing. This is like a rebirth of the energy. I like to observe this. This is like a celebration. Heat energy begins to change and a whole new energy body emerges. That is fascinating.

Do you also do visual operations?

∞

No.

You can now leave a message for the people; what would you like to tell them?

That people have to learn that their energy will live on for a very long time. When they manage to wish to be cleansed in full concentration then they will succeed in doing so. This purity will be rewarded in the cosmos and the levels you can reach through this are bright and beautiful. But if you do not reach purity in life or you destroy this purity, the energy will be too weak and you will not be able to go far into the energy worlds in the phase of your transition. This is then the state of purgatory that you know from your old writings.

You want to appeal to the people to work towards their cleansing every day, is this right?

257

Yes.

After what is known about your lives, it seems that your lifetime in Rome was the period of your worst impurity; do I see this correctly?

Yes, that is correct. Many contaminations happened there. This time was marked by luxury and debauchery. We only lived the ego. There was no other power than the ego. This energy contaminated us and it is very difficult to put into words how the ego can be cleansed. I would need books in order to impart this information. The only thing that can heal these contaminations is love. Love in all of its forms is the healing, also for these contamina-

tions, for everybody that received them in those days.

Can you remember the Roman priestesses that were also called Vestal virgins?

Very little, these women were very peculiar and they were never visible. There were always in their domain. Their task was the cleansing of the flames of truth.

But they cannot have done very well if you were all so badly contaminated?

No, you cannot say it like that; these women were very good at that task. I just did not pay any attention to them, that is all.

Is there anything more you would like to tell the people?

Love is the key to healing. I want to say that this is important, everything else is inconsequential; the cleansing as well is only a form of love, therefore please really impart to them that love is the core and the goal of healing; again and again.

There are people who love another person too much; is that also the kind of love you mean?

No, that is not the kind that I mean. The kind of love I mean is the love for All That Is. That is the answer.

You mean love for all that exists and all that we meet; this love makes us mindful and mindfulness leads to awareness. And this is where energy transformation happens, right?

Yes.

As you are praying so much now, for whom do you pray?

For a wide variety of things; sometimes for the people, sometimes for the world.

And how does it happen that you pray for individual people?

That happens very easily. A person is connected to us and we feel their love. If you call for help, this request reaches us as an energy impulse and I take care of these requests and pray for these people.

259

And what happens to the impulse?

Their energy connects to mine and we start to raise the power inside them; that is the healing.

So this is similar to the process of an operation in which the energy is also being raised?

Yes.

Dear Emanuel, did you want to say anything else?

...You have already asked a lot.

I believe I have no more questions now.

That is well.

May I tell people that they should turn to you when they need support or help in their prayers?

Yes, with pleasure. That is a beautiful idea. Tell them about me and they will do this. They should call on me for help and I will focus the energy and strengthen the connection. This will accelerate the materialization of the prayer's intent.

Yes, I will do this. Well, I thank you many times and I say "until next time."

Until next time.

The Quiet Form

In an interview with Chico Xavier he suggested that I talk to the "Quiet Form", because he felt that it would be important for the people to know about it. So I am now asking to be connected to the Quiet Form.

Interview

Dear Quiet Form, what exactly are you?

I am the form that protects the entities. I dwell in Abadiânia and I am the form that protects this place.

How can I visualize that? How exactly do you protect this place?

It is a kind of frequency, as you call it, I am a kind of frequency that absorbs the energy of the others. This is what you call it, right?

Yes, I mean, are you an entity?

No.

You are an energy field?

Yes; the frequency that I am is the energy that serves to protect this area, it cannot be explained in terms of space. You have to imagine this as an inherent form.

That means that you are everywhere but the quality of this frequency is to prevent negativity from entering this space?

Yes.

Why is this so?

The energies that surround Abadiânia need a lot of strength in order to live. They try to get this strength from Abadiânia, but the frequency of my energy does not allow them to do this.

Then you are, as we like to say, the pinch of salt in the soup, that makes the taste just so, so that those who do not like the salt cannot eat this soup, right?

Yes, exactly.

You are only active in these energy fields here on earth?

Yes, but I am a cosmic power.

So other places do not benefit from this, your protective power?

263

This is like a kind of gestalt that has a shape.

Are you a part of the energy of this place or are you separate from it?

This is a human question; there is no separation...

I wanted to understand if the type of energy that vibrates in Abadiânia always goes along with a form of energy that you are.

Yes.

And why do you think that Chico wanted me to talk to you?

So that the people may know that there is a special kind of pro-

tection here. This is important in order to make the connection possible for them. Most people have fears that block the connection. The people must have faith - they need to trust; otherwise they cannot heal.

Do you have a colour?

...Yes and no; not a colour that you know but you could recognize me as a colour if you could see frequencies. That would then be blue, light blue.

And how do you nourish yourself?

That is not necessary, I just am.

Then I thank you very much.

Thank you.

Dom Ingrid

Interview

I would like to establish contact to the energy perceived by the people as Dom Ingrid.

Dear Dom Ingrid, I would like to get to know you as I have got to know all the other entities that are coming to Abadiânia to incorporate into Joao. May I ask you about your last lifetime?

Yes, with pleasure.

Please tell me where you lived and when?

This time is stored in my memory as the time of cleansing; unfortunately I cannot remember a time that you recognise.

No problem, then let us look into your time of cleansing. Please tell me, did you have a nice childhood as a girl?

Yes I was very well protected especially during my childhood, I am very grateful to my parents for this. This strength that they gave me was very special. Then there began a time of inner reflection that I needed in order to understand who I really was. This time was very important to me and I went into an ecclesiastical institution in order to do this. I spent many years there, which I enjoyed very much, because there as well I enjoyed much protection. It so happened that

∞

one day in the church I perceived the essence of Mary.

How did you perceive it?

The power around Mary became very strong and I knew at that moment: She is with me. Then I spoke to her and she answered. The first question that I had was about the holy sacraments, whether I would be permitted to receive them one day.
Mary answered this with a connection that she showed me in the form of a feeling. I knew that the power that I felt was the divine power of the female. Thus I began to understand that I was to work as a female person, not in a genderless capacity despite being in a female body.

In what way was this the answer to your question about the holy sacraments?

The question was not whether I deserved them but whether I should take them. But her answer was like a path into the world.

And you understood it in this way that she counselled you to walk the path of your power and not to suppress it, the way institutions like that do in the shape of celibacy and other forms of asceticism?

Exactly.

What happened next, what was the next question?

The next question I had was the about the origin of all being, and with that I desired to know where God dwells. She sent me an image again. The predominant energy that I perceived as coming from her was connected to a source that I cannot describe. The power of this source is always there and is ever unchangeable. This I understood as the answer to my question about God, and I realised that God was not of male gender as I had thought; this is why I was ready to take the new steps.

And these were?

The last question I asked of her was the question about the meaning of life. I wanted to know why people always have such a negative outlook on life and why they are unable to go into a positive perception. In answer to this, she sent me a loving hug and began to send this power into my heart. Then I understood that the energy is in our hearts and that many people have very little energy there. This was very easy to understand for me, because I had met people who seemed very cold; at this moment of Mary's hug I knew that there was more warmth in her loving touch than I had hitherto found in people.

267

And what decision did you take after this encounter?

The next few days were rather difficult for me because I realised that my present form was not the right one for me. Human power is limited, yet I wanted to increase this power. This is why I allowed myself to live this energy in the form of love in this form that I have now.

Does this mean that you chose suicide?

Yes.

Oh, that must have been a difficult step because I believe that the church of all institutions would have taken a rather dim view of that?

I could not help but overcome all of this.

Do you think that Mary wanted you to leave this form so quickly?

...Hmm... I wanted to work and to help and I knew that I could not do that in this human form. The world in which I lived was very cold indeed and I would have needed a lot of strength in order to overcome this cold in order to have encountered just one loving person. That was not enough for me.

My I ask you about your passing? What was it like, how did you go into the transition?

Mary's love was my home. I knew where I wanted to go, this was why I was never afraid during that time.

What did you do, how did you die?

That was in the church. I wanted to be with her after I left.

And what exactly did you do?

The doctors helped me with that sleeping medicine. I did not do this with their complicity; I procured these medicines and took them in the church.

∞

Were you all alone at that time? Did you not have a bad conscience vis-à-vis your family?

The family I had was a bridge into this experience. I was in the nunnery most of the time and had not been in contact with my biological family for a long time. It is true that there were questions of conscience, yet my longing for home was so great that I could not help myself. Then began the journey of the soul through the worlds. I knew what Mary's power felt like and therefore I knew exactly where I wanted to go, into which state of being I wanted to go. The first perception was the energy of other people. But these were without the sort of body that we knew (author's note: the deceased). I perceived their energy but I did not see their faces. That was very frightening, but I was able to calm myself. I saw the people in connection with each other and I saw how their hearts were closed. This connection was very weak with most of the people. Then I went on to the next level.

269

I have a quick question – in the level that you just described, what was your environment like; was it light or was it dark there?

The environment where I perceived these human energies was very dark. That was also very frightening.

And what happened then?

The next level was very bright, it was much warmer there and I felt that the love was already stronger in them. There you could also perceive the deceased, but their energy was brighter and of a higher vibration. I knew that they were more connected to the source that the others.

Were there many?

Yes, there were many, I cannot say a number.
And then I went on to the next level, there I found the angels and
fell in love with their power. I knew the angels from the pictures in
the church, but these angels were far more loving. The power that
emanated from them was many times more strongly connected than
we can understand in our earthly perception. The angels were be-
ings of light that appeared in the shape of an orb, but I wanted to
perceive them in the form that I had carried with me all these years.
Then I rose up to the level of the Masters. There I was connected
and I wanted to go further, but I could not. The power that I had was
not enough to rise any higher. That made me a little sad, but I began
to remember that I was capable of sensing the power of Mary, there-
fore I followed this feeling and through this I came into a new per-
ception. The energy that she emanates is not to be found in a form.
It is the power of the female as pure energy.

And what happened then?

This realisation had come to me already in church, but now I
wanted to find this energy form. So I continued to search. I trav-
elled the level of the Masters and searched inside myself whether I
could find this power anywhere. Then there came a moment where
I connected with the power of her loving, exceptionally bright en-
ergy and I suddenly had the power I had not had before and through
that I managed to climb to the next level.

So you were able to change your energy through your intention and the
concentration of all your strength so that your perception changed, and

this is how you were able to find her?

Yes, exactly. Then I arrived on the fourth level. I was now at the level of the Masters of the exceptional Qualities and I knew that here, I could contact her better than before. This is why I began to look further and I found Dom Ignacio.

How did you perceive him?

The energy that he is is warm and bright; for a moment I had thought that it was Mary, but I soon understood that he is Dom Ignacio, and then I observed his work in the world of the humans. I saw him work in the world of the humans although he was here on this level. I did not understand this and therefore I continued to observe. I would never have been able to understand this without help because he is very much preoccupied in his attention

271

What do you mean when you say without help – who helped you?

The power of Valdivino whom I soon began to perceive as well was my deliverance; he was equally full of love and the power of love. I observed Ignacio and Valdivino observed me. That brought him to me and we communicated with each other. In his kind of perception communication still happened in pure thought; this brought me even more strongly into the connection with him, so that I wanted to understand it even more. This type of communication was strange to me, but I knew that it was right. Then I slowly understood how Dom Ignacio performed this work and I also wanted to be involved in it. Therefore I began to go to the place where he worked in the world of humans. This once made me also go into the body of Joao, but I could not bear this energy. I needed expansion and therefore I decided to stay connected with this level; but I will not go into a body.

So you only direct your attention now without descending all the way, as we would say?

Yes.

Are you also present during invisible operations?

Yes, this type of operation as you call it is very helpful for the souls and I like to be present when I can help.

Dear Dom Ingrid, and are you now happier than when you were in a human body?

Yes.

And do you have any idea why you had even come to earth at that time?

Yes, that was the process of cleansing. I need the energy in order to find expansion.

What made you feel most constricted?

The rules of the humans... especially the monastic rules. This power is not healthy in its very idea, because it separates the people from the actual area of effect. This energy is never separated, and that is why help through prayer especially is not human, but I find it diffi-

cult to find the words for this.

I understand; you want to say that these forms generally may be okay for a limited time, but not forever, because they divide what is not truly divided, right?

> *Yes, that is about it; the people's spheres of effect should meld and not work separately from each other. Is that easier to understand?*

Yes; I did understand, do not worry. But generally the monastery was good as a place of protection?

> *Yes, but the limited framework there is not beneficial. I would have loved to have the possibility to change that. The insights were so profound that I could not stay there any longer. That is proof enough how I felt, isn't it?*

273

Yes I understand, most of all you felt powerless because you saw what should be changed but you couldn't change anything, right?

> *Yes.*

How do you perceive the people now from this level?

> *The people are still very cold in their hearts, but I always bring them love when I touch them, this opens their hearts and it is healing...*

How do you touch them?

The people only need attention and I give it to them.

Do you also go into the rooms of the Casa in order to do this?

Yes.

Is there something that makes you sad when you work here?

Yes... the people get so much strength from us and then they squander it again. That is sometimes a little sad, but I am not of a sad nature, therefore please take these words not too literally in relation to their human meaning.

I do understand you; don't worry. You just think it is a pity, right?

274

Yes, exactly.

And what makes you glad?

The people, when they heal. That is really wonderful to watch, then I am as glad inside as if I were a little girl back in those days. That is always very nice.

You know I have the possibility to leave the people a message. If you would like to do that, then please begin...

With pleasure: The love in us is the key to the source. The women have to open their hearts in order to love the men, and the men, in order to love the women. The value of this power cannot be described with words. The realisation that God is not a person who

∞

directs everything, but is a source of power that directs everything, makes the importance of the male and female in your forms all the more significant. This is very important to me: that people come into their power. The love of God is not the love for a man or a being; the love of God is the connection to everything.

And did you manage to find the power of Mary on your search?

That is a good question. I have found her power in myself – that is the answer. You will find the answer to all questions IN YOURSELF. That is the simple truth.

Dear Dom Ingrid, would you like to say anything else?

No.

275

Then I thank you very much for the wonderful insights into your perception. Again, we have learned many interesting and connecting things. Thank you for being and thank you for working like this. See you soon.

See you soon.

Eso, the entity in the garden

Since all energy has consciousness, it is possible that we are being contacted by energy gestalts that are different from those we are already familiar with, for example in the form of the departed or the so-called angels or the Masters. I happened to meet one such different gestalt one day when I was sitting in the Casa's garden and an unfamiliar presence was contacting me.

Interview

Who are you?

> *I am Eso.*

Please describe to me what exactly you are.

> *I am the energy entity that you can find in the garden. I am very close to the energy of the plants. It is my task to soothe the people in their exhaustion.*

Entity of Eso: Are you alone or are there other helpers at your side?

> *There are no others of this quality here in the garden.*

What advice can we give the people who wish to come into contact with you?

> *When they are here in the garden they should call Eso and ask that we be connected.*

Dear entity of Eso, how did you find your way here, how did you get here?

> *I am only in the garden, I am always where plants grow.*

How did you get here – to this place?

I wanted to help at a place where actual connection is possible.

How did you find this place?

I felt the wish to experience the expansion of the cosmos in all its splendour. So (author's note: through this wish) begins the movement and this movement has brought me here. The energy of this place is really unique. If you can, it is possible here to come into contact with the source of all being. That is how pure and exceptional this place is.

Why? Is there a reason why this place is so pure?

For many thousands of years a ladder into the higher levels has existed here. There are different components to the energy of this place. It is the cosmic placement. This place is one of the purest places in the whole of the cosmos. It is not the purest place in the whole universe, but it is the purest place on earth.

278

What does this purity look like?

The energy fields are clean. What happens when a person comes here who obviously has not grown up in purity and then dives into this purity? When a human being is contaminated, the fields are being cleansed one after the other. Thus begins a process that sets many things in motion and connects the soul with the state of the all-purifying source. This dissolves the causes for the illness; like a direct connection into the cause of the illness. Still this part is not a fast path, however direct it appears to be.

Dear Eso, what else would you like to tell me?

I am connected to the earth and I am working through it.

Dear Eso, how am I to imagine you?

I am an energy field that fills the whole garden. Wherever the earth is visible, there I am.

How far does your influence extend? 1 metre, 2 metres, 3 metres, 4 metres…?

In your measurements my influence extends about 2 metres above the surface of the earth.

You are an energy field that can be invoked directly – and what can we ask you for in our invocation?

279

I cleanse the people through the quality of my energy.

What else would you like to share with the people who will be reading this?

The real cleansing of the people happens inside them, not outside of them, but here they will find the necessary environment in order to perform the cleansing of the inside.

Then I thank you many times, dear Eso, and I am looking forward to the next time when I am sitting in the garden asking you for cleansing. Thank you.

I thank you.

280

Practical

∞

282

Casa Guide

Interview

Who would like to talk to me about the questions in the Casa guide?

I would be happy to answer your questions. I am Dom Ignacio.

Dear Dom Ignacio, I am very happy that you have come forth.

I am happy too. By now, you have become familiar with many of us. That is good and I am happy when the messages are written to go out into the world.

I would like to ask you a few questions about the Casa.
First of all, the equilateral triangle, can you explain to us what it stands for?

Yes, the triangle is the balancing energy that is initiated here to be given into the path of the souls. The energy that transforms. This is the primary message, because with that everything has been said about what happens here.

When the humans pray to the triangle, what or whom should they be praying to?

That does not matter; the only thing that is important is that they

concentrate the energy they wish to transform.

Why do you have to wear white clothing here?

The white clothing is necessary so that we can get into the layers more easily; this is purely a matter of energy.

So white clothing is conducive to openness.

Yes.

And black clothing closes off?

Yes.

Why is the triangle pointing upwards, not downwards?

The upward pointing triangle is the connection into the higher levels.

Why should you not wear a belt?

Because metal confuses the energy.

Are you allowed to wear rings…?

A few rings are okay, but not to excess.

Why are you not supposed to cross your arms or legs?

This would block the flow of energy, which we actually want to accelerate.

What happens if you knot your clothing?

Then it is not quite so intense, but still.

Why are you supposed to close your eyes in the Current room?

The energy in the Current room is very highly elevated and when the eyes are closed during this process, you will absorb more of this energy. When the eyes are open you absorb less and you are distracted.

Why is it recommended to stay in this place?

285

This is simply the energetic signature of the place; it is only here that the shining orbs have an especially strong effect.

There are people who say that when you leave the Casa, you can encounter much negativity.

Yes, that is true and this is quite normal because you can find the usual negative fields there. Basically, the energy of the earth is contaminated and therefore needs special places in order to vibrate in purity.

Why is silence so important here?

This is the key to healing. The healing energy that we give into the souls here is especially high. The energy needs time to penetrate the layers that surround the human being. This is all very internal and the silence supports this inwardness and preserves the energy. Communication would achieve the opposite.

What exactly would you like to tell me about the prescribed period of rest after the operation?

The 40 days are a symbolic number so that people can get a feeling for how long this process takes. It is always different; sometimes it can take even longer than these 40 days, just as it can be shorter.

How will the people know when the process is finished?

The energy will be steadily elevated inside them and on the day that they feel that they are in their full power, the process is finished. But because most people do not feel when they are receiving those impulses, the 40 days are exactly right in any case.

What happens in the waiting room?

In there, there are the initial entities of cleansing that start to cleanse the aura. These are shining orbs that do this work.

Can the patient accelerate the process there?

The people there can call the energies and ask for cleansing; then the process begins, until they step before the entity.

And they will be cleansed along the whole way?

∞

There will be preparations until it is time, but many people bring much contamination with them so that it will take the entire time to prepare the fields.

Then what happens on the way?

In the hall there is the energy of the shining orbs.
Then the queue begins to raise the energy more and more. With every step, the energy rises. Then, when you stand before the entity, the energy is at its highest point. The special thing there is that the energy there is twice as high as it was before that last step.... sometimes even many times as high.

Is this because we are then stepping into your aura?

Yes.

What about the shining orbs along the path?

The shining orbs are also there the whole time; their effect there is more intense on the people who meditate.

What happens in the room next to Joao?

There the energy is also still very high. I would rather describe this as an intermediary level. You very slowly come down out of the very high energy.

What about the operation room?

There the energy is also very high, but not as high as before Joao.

What happens in the Current room?

The people are further cleansed by the shining orbs. This is a very elaborate process and needs a lot of time, that is why it is good that they meditate a lot. You know by now how the shining orbs work.

Will many meditations have the same effect as an operation?

No, the operation is a very special thing. There, we give more energy than can ever be given by the shining orbs... this is a very cosmic thing.

It is written in the Casa Guide that the cleansing will take place in the first room of the Current, is this correct?

Not quite, because the shining orbs expand the soul/the energy body, so that the entity can see faster and better what exactly the energetic status of the person is.

So the shining orbs have a cleansing effect and they make the light bodies softer and wider?

Yes, that is correct.

And that only happens in the first room?

In the second room the energy is slowly elevated, this makes the expansion even softer, in other words like a fruit that is left to ripen a bit longer.

I have once heard it called the room of the spiritual entities?

The spiritual entities here are incorporated into Joao and the shining orbs are also here... those are all spiritual entities.

What should we call these rooms?

These rooms there are all exclusively rooms of acceleration.

What happens in the back room?

There are also operations performed there and the energy there is also still very high.

289

There doesn't seem to be a transition; you suddenly find yourself outside of the rooms after an operation. It is as if you "fell" out of this room in a way.

And that is correct; that is still a thorn in my side; I do not like that. The people need a better catchment room, a closed room would be more helpful because the energies are quickly being distracted away from you by all of the outer circumstances of the nature and of the many people that are immediately all around you.

How do you perceive the rooms? Do you see the rooms or the people?

The rooms we see as enclosed spaces of protection that enclose your auras when we work there. This is good and important.

∞

What happens in the recovery room?

The people lie down there and are being worked on by the shining orbs. That can happen very quickly or take some time.

What exactly happens in the revision line?

There we check whether the internal energies have really improved.

Do you remember how the person in question looked previously?

It is visible when somebody is going through a process, whether they want to heal or whether they are blocking the healing.

290

So when somebody is sent back from the revision line to have another operation, this means that they have blocked the process?

Yes. The revision should be a separate session that is not governed by a further operation. Mostly, that is only the case when healing does not happen in the desired way.

Is there something that you would like to tell the people who have made their way here? According to some texts, contact with you is already initiated earlier (for instance in the aeroplane).

That is correct, we perceive the resonances; who wants to come; as soon as the decision has been made, we serve the aim, that means we begin to initiate the process by slowly preparing the energy of the body for the kind of intervention we are performing here.

How do you prepare them?

We expand them. This is like a plant that is still in a small pot, and this process is rather like the preparation that we make. Then, the arrival in Abadiânia is like the expansion into the large flowerpot.

So you slowly pour in energy?

Yes.

And this "pouring with energy" only happens because the people make the decision?

It is not as easy as that. The energy flows because the people are opening up and they do this only after making the decision to do so.

291

But this would mean that the people only have to open up, no matter where they are on earth, and then this expansion will begin?

No, not really; the concentration of energy here is unique, therefore you cannot make a direct comparison. Everyone can always connect to us. But whether they will understand us or whether we will really reach them through the many layers of the Earth's magnetism is another question.

Why do you have to lay your hand on the place where the operation is to take place?

That is a misinformation... The hand actually complicates the op-

eration; please communicate this!

Then where are they supposed to lay [their hands]?

> *The hands should always lie next to the body with their palms open*
> *so that the energy can flow, eyes closed.*
> *When people lie in their beds, their hands should also be lying palm*
> *up, next to the body.*

What can you tell me about the length of the operations?

> *The operations do not need much time, the process itself is a thing*
> *of seconds; therefore even a minute of your time would be sufficient.*
> *The proper healing is happening in a completely different place in*
> *a completely different state of being afterwards.*

292

Now I have a few questions about the guidelines for the time after the operation given in the official Casa Guide.

Resting for 24 hours after the operation is important?

> *Yes, very. Better even longer afterwards.*

What can you tell me about physical exertion?

> *Physical exertion is not advisable. It is like a concentrated direct*
> *charging up of the body; this requires much rest and time.*

What about the power of the sun after an operation?

∞

The sun is power and when you have been through the stress of an operation, you first of all need rest. The power of the sun is then much too much energy for a system that has already received a lot of energy through the operation. The operation is very intense. Some people could become overloaded through the firing up by the sun's energy, which after all does not only consist of light as you know it.

You should not seek the company of many people, but rest?

The cleansing needs rest and this process takes a lot of time. Communicating with other people takes a lot of strength; therefore it is not good for the process of healing. The entities have already said much about this; I hope it gets through to you how important this point is.

You are not supposed to leave the house for 24 hours?

Yes, this is about the rest and the lying down... Some people take a long time in order to get up and to move. Therefore we have specified rest for 24 hours.

You are banned from the Casa for a day?

This is so because the energies of negativity are being soaked up here and transformed by the shining orbs, but the shining orbs are not always at hand when negative energy fields move, and therefore it is important for you not to go into the Casa during this time. These energy fields could induce a change in your fields again.

∞

Wouldn't it then make more sense to tell people to dress in black?

Yes, but I do not want this, because there are too many wrong associations attached to such clothing.

And is it enough to stay away from the Casa for one day?

This is a purely psychological period. The negative energies cannot stay here that long but the people also need this time in order to feel themselves again and to listen to themselves; to feel themselves. Therefore it is better that they stay away for a whole day and so not run into problems with the remaining old energy fields here.

No sport and no strenuous exercise for eight days afterwards? Only eight days?

This is a symbolic number; everything connected to the number eight is connected to healing. It is different for everyone when their healing process is finished; therefore the people have to listen to themselves in order to better understand the healing impulses. But eight days are a nice guideline and give the right shape to the whole thing.

No sex?

This kind of energy has no place here.

About the revision after the eight days: Why should you wear white clothing in bed?

∞

That is not necessary, it is just a form that is supposed to help peo-
ple to find a connection to this place, it does need a special con-
centration and people are better able to attain this via such visual
support.

Why the glass of water next to the bed?

The energy that we connect is very pure and for this, we need new
energy. This water absorbs the pure energy of healing and when
people drink this water it is a form of energy that they take in.

And through this, the people get their strength back?

Yes, exactly.

Why water?

Because it is the easiest substance to program.

We are supposed to ask you to remove the stitches?

Others do this; I am at that point already engaged with looking after
the souls further, insofar that I begin to further expand the energy.

So who removes the stitches?

The shining orbs.

What exactly do they do? Do they really remove stitches?

∞

*No, they connect; the energy of the people is then a little more ele-
vated and we reconnect this energy again. The whole thing is like
a new kind of cleansing.*

Why do you have to say the prayer before drinking in the morning?

You know this…
(Author's note: Please read the chapter about "Praying and wishing in
the Casa".)

About the *herbs* – which task do they perform from your perspective?

*Herbs are different products that are supposed to calm the body.
This is simply necessary in order to remove your tension and this
relaxation helps to accelerate the expansion of the soul.*

296

Why are you not allowed to eat pork?

*This is another thing which is purely energetic. Pigs have the habit
of eating a lot of negativity. Unfortunately this is part of their ge-
netic programming; they do not distinguish. They take up this negativity into their meat and it remains there. This is the reason why
you are not supposed to eat pork during this time, because through
this food you absorb the negativity of these animals.*

Why are you not supposed to drink alcohol during this time?

*This is easy to answer; because alcohol clouds perception, and we
want to work towards clarifying perception.*

Why are you not supposed to eat pepper during this time?

This spice also clouds perception; therefore it is not advisable.

How do you know this?

I see it.

How?

The people who eat such things and who live in this way have a contaminated perception.

What about the blessed water? Why has it been blessed?

The energy of the place is absorbed by the water, therefore it is blessed as you call it. In actual fact it has only been energised. That happens relatively quickly, but often the bottles here are several days old and therefore they have been energised in any case.

297

Do you have to use that water; is it not sufficient to pray over the water?

*No, the energy is lost as soon as you leave the place. The energy is gone as quickly as it came into the water **and** it is quite right to communicate to the people that they can charge the water through the prayers.*

Could you use any type of water at home?

You have different types of water; people should enquire where to obtain the purest water, uncarbonated and without metals.

Concerning the crystal beds: Why do you have to chose an uneven number of sessions?

This is a type of superstition with Joao; it has nothing to do with energy.

Should the people lie on the crystal bed more than once?

Yes, the cleansing of the chakras is an integral part of the healing process, therefore every day that people lie on the crystal beds is a day gained in the healing process.

298

Why is it important to be barefoot when you step before the triangle in the casa?

This is simply a matter of energy because you can pray or wish better when connected directly with the earth... This energy is simply stronger when it flows directly through you and not through shoes.

Why do you have to touch the triangle on the floor with your forehead?

It is a symbolic thing: the human head touching the triangle or the wall in the triangle only serves to make them feel more keenly what they do.

What about the rose prayer?

∞

The prayer is very beautiful because it releases really beautiful energies. These energies in turn create other beautiful resonances; this is a beautiful and quite unimportant process for the entire universe.

Why should you not receive any other healing methods after the operation?

The other healing methods interfere with the person's aura. Because this is wide open, and because you could never foresee which energies a healer will bring along; this is why we categorically say it is best not to employ other healing methods.

You should also refrain from calling on other levels because it interferes with the healing process. It is important that the people remain with themselves entirely and do not enter into any belief patterns during this time.

299

What can you say about the waterfall? What exactly is the significance of the waterfall?

The waterfall is a symbolic cleansing for the people, but there are also entities there; you have experienced this already. The waterfall can mainly be used for mental cleansing.

Please bear in mind that the entities of a specific place are able to heal best in that place, therefore it is advisable to call on the entities dwelling there and not on us.

∞

The Crystal beds

Interview

Dear Entities of Healing, I would like to ask you a few questions about the crystal beds now. What exactly happens there; and what do you do there? I would like you to tell me about this.

With pleasure.

Then please tell me what exactly you do in the crystal bed.

We're cleansing the chakras one after the other, starting with the lower ones, then steadily working our way up until we have reached the last chakra at the top; then we revive the soul's energy with one last impulse, and then our work is done.

Is this what you always do?

Yes, we always do this.

Then I would like to understand why these crystals are needed and why the colours?

These crystals accelerate our possibility to go into the chakras; they simplify our work.

And what if people were using such crystal beds elsewhere on earth?

That is not really a problem, because then the crystals are also cleansing in their fashion. The whole thing then just happens a little more slowly.

How many of you are at work on such an occasion?

Most people lie down and at once we start our work. The number is undetermined. It depends on the mass of the energy that we have to move.

That means that we have to imagine it like this: that very many orbs are around us then?

Yes.

301

What happened to me once was that I fell asleep whilst you were doing this. Why does that happen?

The tiredness of the soul is the energy that determines the path of this healing.

What do you mean when you say tiredness of the soul?

The purity of a soul determines its alertness. And when a person is very tired they fall asleep very quickly. The purity there is not so high.

Does this mean that the more awake you feel, the purer you are?

This is correct. But you have to distinguish; this alertness is not the alertness of the spirit inside you, the alertness of the spirit is the mind; the alertness of the soul is the power of the soul.

Then why do I always feel so out of sorts after that?

This is the power of your soul; you feel the power inside you much more clearly.

That means the tension in my body can no longer mask this power?

Yes, exactly.

Compared to the operations, what is the difference between your work here and the operations?

The cleansing in the crystal beds is many times more gentle; therefore it is much easier for many people to walk this path; because they are basically of the speed of your spirits and will not become very highly accelerated.

Perhaps you could also say that many crystal bed sessions are like an operation?

You could say that, but it is not directly comparable, because the beds only accelerate the chakras, but the operations go deeply into the soul; this means that in the operations you can be more easily connected to your soul's energy than in the crystal bed. There, it happens on the physical level through the chakras. The chakras are close to your body; the operations that happen on the energetic level transform the energy of the soul.

One spiritual entity told me that you are like a kind of pyramid that reaches into our visible sky, is this correct?

Yes, that is correct.

And Dr. Augusto said that you also work in England.

This is partly correct, we are not in all places there, but we have our favourite places on earth.

For example?

Cambridge Cathedral and of course many other places.

303

Are you all connected with each other... also with the orbs over there?

What a question, yes, we are all connected.

Do you have a message for us?

The power of the sun is far more special than you believe. You can tell the people that the energy coming from the sun is more than the things that you can perceive. This energy is in the power of the source.

Does this have a connection to the source?

The sun represents this power in visual form; this is easier for you

to understand. The sun in its vibration is not just material in nature. The energy that is being created in the sun is also spiritual; the energy that it sends out as rays of light is material. Those two components allow you to live.

And what can I tell people?

That they can connect with the power of the sun; then they accelerate their healing by many times.

Is it important that this happens at such a pure place as this or is it the same everywhere?

It is better at a pure place because the fields of communication with the spiritual sun can reach this place here in better connectedness. The sun is visible for you everywhere, but is not accessible everywhere in all its purity.

That means that spiritually it is most easily accessible via a pure place.

Yes, exactly.

What do we tell the people, how can they best reach the sun?

We just have to concentrate on its power, not look into the sun, nor look in its direction; it is enough to direct consciousness there.

Does this also work inside a room?

It does not matter; the important thing is the purity of the place.

∞

That means you connect with this power of the sun.

The energy of the sun begins to invigorate your spiritual bodies.

Dear white orbs, how many of you are now here with me?

You cannot count us.

And you also work on the people when they just sit here and rest?

No.

So you only work in the crystal beds and during the operations?

Yes, the cleansing in the crystal beds and during the operations are our fields of activity.

I have been told that people have been protecting themselves from the sun after an operation, what do you have to say about this?

This is correct, because the spiritual energy of the sun can have a very accelerating effect on some people, and that can overload their energy system, this is also very important.
We are the helping hands that serve in the areas next to the operation rooms, and we love to help.
People can establish contact with us when they are better able to call us; therefore it is good and well that you all pass on this information to them. The people have to learn that they can reach us through their consciousness and that they should learn that we hear them, always!

∞

Is it important to speak this request or is it enough to think it?

It is enough to call us in thought. The energy is the important point, not the word.

But that would mean that you are able to read every person's thoughts?

This is the case in principle, but we are only concerned with the people's calls, not with their other thoughts.

So when they concentrate on you more this connection will be strengthened?

Yes, exactly.

306

I thank you very much for this beautiful information.

∞

The Waterfall

Interview

Dear entities, I am here at the waterfall and would like to know what we can tell the people about this waterfall in order for them to better connect with you?

At the beginning of their path, the people have to ask the entities of love to accompany them. This path will then become symbolically the path of love. The people must call upon the entities of cleansing; this is best at the place where you have got the waiting area, on the path to the waterfall... down below where the door is.

What should they observe when they call upon the entities of cleansing?

The energy of this place is very pure...
The people should ask that the different layers of their aura and therefore their body be involved in a special cleansing. That is then the next step.

What happens next when they walk through the door?

There please call upon the entity of cleansing. The entities are all always here, but you can only call upon one entity after another for the most part.

∞

What happens when they are on the path and arrive at the first bridge?

There they should stop and reflect. The energy of the people is very closely linked to awareness, therefore it is important that they become aware and at the same time reflect upon the past.

Then they walk over the bridge; should they ask something whilst doing that?

The entities of change are already there with them; this means that they can ask for everything they want to change in their old energy.

Then after the first bridge, what happens then?

Then they are in the next area. There the entity of change is waiting for them; this means now that the words that they have just spoken are immersed into this energy.

That means everything that they have just become aware of and spoken out loud will now be transformed.

Yes.

And now they should explicitly call upon the entity of change?

Yes.

*The time of **changing their clothes** they can use in order to let the reflection of the old things operate upon them a little longer.*

Then comes the path down to the waterfall...

There they should then ask the entity of change to bring the words that were spoken into their balance, these words are still filled with emotions, this means that they must transform the emotions in order to make the energy capable of being transformed.

Then you come to the second bridge, what happens then?

There please call the entity of rebirth. The energy wants to be re-born here.

It was transmitted to me that the people should also give thanks here at the bridge.

This is true, but it is also important that they ask for new energy for the future...

309

So they are standing at the bridge, and now they are asking for the re-birth?

Yes.

Should they concentrate on their words and thoughts the whole time?

Yes; then please proceed across the bridge and stay mentally with these wishes, then continue on to the next bridge.

What does this part signify?

∞

This is the path into the strength.

Whom or what are they supposed to call on now?

Nobody there; but when you have arrived at the next bridge please ask the entity of connection; that takes a little time and therefore it is important that you really stay long in this place. Please just ask to be reconnected.

Then they walk across the bridge while asking to be connected. What comes next?

Then you walk into the waterfall; there various other entities are waiting for the people. Here the wishes of the people will be taken in and transformed.

310

What should they do here? Who should they call upon?

The strength of the person determines whom they can call upon here. The best possibility to reach all of them is to call upon all of them one after another.
The entity of love,
of cleansing,
of healing,
of transformation,
of vitality,
of connection.

Are there shining orbs at the waterfall?

∞

Yes; just a few, but there are some.
But the concentration should be upon the entities.

Can you send me an image of how the entities work there at the waterfall?

Most of these forces are oval light energies, as you would call
them.

Can you also connect with spirits of nature here?

You can; but not everybody can deal with these powers.

What should the people ask these entities for?

The people can ask every entity for healing; then these processes
begin to flow into their aura.
The energy fields are injected into the people's auras via the sensa-
tion of the flowing water.

311

Is this water special water?

No.

I once received the information that this waterfall also symbolically
stands for the flow of life.

Yes, this flow is the energy that flows continuously, and whoever is
connected to it is connected with all energies.

∞

What should the people visualise when they walk into the water?

They should imagine how the water cleanses their bodies. The soul remains part of it and therefore will also be cleansed.

What else would you like to tell the people?

At the end of the worship and the appeal people should cross themselves in an upward direction in front of their body; that will connect them. The power of cleansing is the strongest power that they need; the power of transformation is the next power that they need; the power of love is also very important, as is the power of healing. These forces are here for evermore, people can call upon them whenever they want and use their energy. Love is the path. Everything that you offer up for transformation here will be materialized; everything will be transformed here.

312

I thank you very much for all this information; I will pass it all on faithfully.

We thank you also.

Prayer and wishes in the Casa

Instruction

Here are a few small instructions for praying and wishing in the Casa. After several entities pointed out that the energy in the chapel is of a very high vibration, I have assembled a few guidelines about prayer and wishing in the chapel with their help.

1) Write your wish on a piece of paper, clearly and to the point. Express your wish as simply and directly as possible. If you have more than one wish, use a new piece of paper for every whish.

2) Draw the sign of a horizontal figure of eight, the symbol of eternity, after each wish.

3) Enter the chapel.

4) Step before the triangle, holding the piece of paper in your right hand.

5) With your left hand, put the tips of thumb and forefinger together to form a mudra. Hold your hand palm up in front of your navel, the elbow bent at a right angle.

6) Now direct all your attention to the piece of paper in your right hand and speak your wish out loud. The energy of your spo-

ken words will now connect with the written words on the paper. Please take care to formulate your wish in accordance with the cosmic law. First and foremost, it must never harm nor hurt another being.

7) When you have spoken your wish and feel that the connection with the piece of paper has been established, hold the paper in front of your body at a distance of about 30 to 40 cm. Here, certain distinctions apply:

a) If you are asking for material abundance, hold the paper in front of your third eye,

b) If you are asking for abundance for your loved ones, hold it in front of your heart,

c) If you are asking for your own abundance, touch the paper with your mouth.

314

8) Try and feel exactly what is happening when you hold the paper in the specified position. You should feel a strong current of energy. This is the establishment of a connection that will bring the written words and the spoken words into a flow of energy. This is the beginning of their materialization; this is how energy fields are created that cause resonances – this is the moment when they begin to work.

9) When you feel that the moment has come, that the connection has been established and that everything is proceeding along its proper path, place the paper into the triangle.

10) Say your thanks and slowly walk backwards out of the chapel.

If you wish to work with photographs, proceed with them one by one just as described above for the pieces of paper. Make sure to hold the photograph in front of your heart (when you ask for others). If you are asking for yourself, touch the photograph with your mouth.

Commentary by Chico Xavier:

What happens when you wish and pray in the chapel?

> *The energy in the chapel is very pure: it is connected to our energies. That makes your words flow directly into our level. We can therefore perceive this energy more easily and pass it on into the fields of resonances.*

But I also had a feeling that a connection was established to my heart and to my third eye. How do you explain that?

> *All energy is always connected to each other; you know this. The wishes that you formulate over there are beginning to materialise.*

So this is like the birth of an energy field?

> *Yes and no. You cannot give birth to energy but you can shape it and direct its consciousness. Nothing is ever newly created but just given a new form; like the words that come out of you have been just formed by you. The energy arises out of your own power and is then **connected** to other forms of energy. It is like modelling clay that has always been there but is now through your power being given a form. You may make another form out of another piece, but both*

forms have always been created out of the same energy.
The question is not where this energy comes from; it always origi-
nates from source. Therefore you have to be careful when you use the
word birth; the energy is only being shaped; it is not newly created.

And out of which components are these energy fields created?

These energy fields come from the energy that you are. Everyone
directs a part of their power and their attention there and sends
this power into the spiritual realms so that it may one day become
matter. It is therefore a connection of your energy to the energy of
the cosmos. The power that comes into being then is a new energy
gestalt, but it is still just energy that has always been there; like a
flower that just develops more leaves. This is hopefully the right
image.

316

Does this mean that human beings create energy fields through their
wishes?

Yes.

And the purity of the source can accelerate this process?

Yes, exactly, this is the reason that the wishes there in the chapel
can be materialized very well through us. This is like a direct wire
to our ears.

Does this mean that if I wish to contact you collectively, that this would
be the best place to go?

∞

Yes.

Why did it sometimes connect with the heart and sometimes with the third eye?

The wishes that need our heart energy are being brought into the heart energy; the wishes that need more help from the world of matter are being directed by the energy of the third eye.

What exactly happens in the triangle on the stage in the hall compared to the triangle in the chapel?

There the energy that is you will be connected with the energy of these human beings.

Then what exactly is your work in that moment, when this connection is being established or strengthened?

While you speak there, the energy begins to take shape and we are directing these fields.

So when a person is praying or formulating wishes, does the result then depend on the strength of his soul?

No, it does not, because we will take up and work upon and direct the wish in every respect; but the souls who are very powerful can of course contribute their strength so that this can happen more easily.

Do you see the people when they stand before the triangle?

We do not see your material form, but we surely feel you very strongly.

I thank you very much for your loving input.

Thank you.

Epilogue

Much of what we think we know can look quite different from the vantage point of a different perception. But how will we perceive things when we have left this human form to change into another? The contamination of your soul can be cleansed through the power of love; I hope that you have learnt how important it is to always be mindful and to open your heart. Every moment counts.

The purity and the incorruptible clarity of the spiritual entities will forever be a guideline for me whenever people suffering from an illness or problem lose themselves in excuses why they have as yet failed to get into balance.

It is the magic of life to recognize that love is a power greater than everything we have ever known or will ever know, and above all imbued with more healing power than all the medicines made by human hands. We are the creators of our own destiny, each and every day, in every single moment of our lives. Claiming responsibility for ourselves is the great test of our lifetime and when we realise this, we will be richly rewarded with love, abundance and energy. None of this can ever be bought with money; everything is already there inside us and is ours to claim. We only have to realise it. There is a host of spiritual entities waiting to help us along the way – we only have to call them.

In love and connectedness
Sylvia Leifheit

PS: I would like to keep this work alive – please do not hesitate to contact me if I have not answered some questions that you might have. I will try to include the answers in the next edition: contact@silverline-publishing.com

"There are no limits beyond those self-imposed by our perception."

Sylvia Leifheit